'This is a deep, wise book. It really ⟨...⟩ it means today to live in the spirit ⟨...⟩ to be very personal and to open up ⟨...⟩ ring true for many others. I especia⟨...⟩ suffering, friendship and joy, but his richest reflections are on how to live with the Jesus who sets us free from worries about our status, position or esteem in the world's eyes.'

Professor David Ford, University of Cambridge

'Written and organized with clarity, the "following" of Christ is here explained as an "easy-hard" way, a matter of change, occasional insights of spiritual vision, and seeing things differently. Marked by attention to joy, silence, friendship, gentleness and humility, struggling "saints" find the courage to take their own perspectives seriously. The implications for all religious institutions are considerable. A profound and accessible book.'

Professor Ann Loades, University of Durham

' "God is not duped by superficial things", Jeff Astley tells us. There is so much here to help us understand the personal nature of faith: poetry, philosophy, plenty of engagement with ordinary life, and indeed equal engagement with the author's own personality. Christ shares our ordinariness and overturns status. This is Christianity at its freshest, most challenging and most stimulating. This is true Christian apologetics.'

The Rt Revd Stephen Platten, Bishop of Wakefield

'Readers . . . will find that they are engaged by a spiritual journal which is wide-ranging, deeply personal and clearly centred on Jesus Christ.'

Professor David Jenkins, former Bishop of Durham

'A true theologian knows how to marry knowledge to experience. Jeff Astley does this to great effect. He is not afraid of what he calls "personal anecdotal theology". He writes from the heart and speaks to the heart . . . His sensitivity to suffering and pain is a particularly strong feature of . . . a wise and humane book. I commend it whole-heartedly.'

The Very Revd Michael Sadgrove, Dean of Durham

'*Christ of the Everyday* weaves together insights from scripture, history, and contemporary culture to provoke new questions about how we might encounter Christ in our complex world. This down-to-earth book is as accessible as it is profound. As Jeff Astley reflects on Christian faith in relation to the joys and struggles of everyday life, readers will find much to challenge their thinking, and even more to enrich their spiritual journey.'

Dr John Drane, author of *The McDonaldization of the Church*

'I have read and greatly appreciated [the book]. It is, as I might have expected, thoughtful and accessible, challenging and provoking, often amusing and sometimes moving. I [am] delighted to commend it.'

Dr John Inge, Bishop of Huntingdon

'We are very fortunate to be given these personal reflections on faith by an experienced Christian educator and theologian. In this book he has sifted an enormous amount of reflection and produced some-thing accessible and welcoming to the interested reader.'

Dr Peter Selby, Bishop of Worcester

'[The book] is relaxed and candid, which wins the reader's confid-ence – and friendship too, I'd say. But it faces difficult problems four square – especially "The only problem" as Muriel Spark called human suffering: [the] chapter on that is particularly good.'

The Very Revd John Drury, Chaplain, All Souls College, Oxford

CHRIST OF THE EVERYDAY

Jeff Astley

First published in Great Britain in 2007

Society for Promoting Christian Knowledge
36 Causton Street
London SW1P 4ST

British Library Cataloguing-in-Publication Data
A catalogue record for this book is available from the British Library

ISBN 978–0–281–05880–8

1 3 5 7 9 10 8 6 4 2

Typeset by Graphicraft Ltd, Hong Kong
Printed in Great Britain by Bookmarque Ltd, Croydon, Surrey.

This book is dedicated to my sons,
Owen and Conrad,
with love

Contents

Introduction

Beginning at the beginning

It was their first session and, being new, they were all eager to take the discussion seriously. Being students at a theological college they also wanted to show themselves worthy of the weighty concerns of Christian theology and ministry. However, the question rather took them aback: 'What makes someone a Christian?'

Everyone felt constrained to come up with an appropriately sophisticated answer. 'A Christian is a person who believes that . . .'; 'A Christian is someone involved in . . .'; 'A Christian is a person who shows the virtues of . . .'; 'A Christian is someone who behaves in such a way that . . .'.

Fortunately, I don't recall my own effort at a definition, only the tutor's quiet response: 'Well, let's look at what Jesus said.' And then the words of the familiar text, suddenly illuminated with a new – and, frankly, rather embarrassing – significance:

> As Jesus passed along the Sea of Galilee, he saw Simon and his brother Andrew casting a net into the lake – for they were fishermen. And Jesus said to them, 'Follow me . . .' And immediately they left their nets and followed him.

(Mark 1.16–18)

Not, apparently, 'Believe all this; understand all that; perform all these religious actions; behave in all these moral ways. And make sure that you are a person with this character.' Not at the beginning, anyway. The Christian, first of all, is the one who *follows*.

So Christianity is both simple and hard. The Christian response and journey are, at base, quite straightforward things. We do not require intellectual sophistication to understand them, nor any superior moral or spiritual stature before we may engage in them. The Christian gospel is not reserved for the clever, the morally squeaky-clean or those who are culturally up-market. Christianity is more ordinary and more every-day than that; and in many ways it is a lot easier than that.

And yet, although it is such an uncomplicated thing to discern and respond to, the call of the gospel is likely to lead us along some very demanding terrain, if we allow it to do so. Much may be demanded of us spiritually and morally; and those who are willing to take it seri-ously intellectually will find themselves engaged in a lot of strenuous reflection as well. In all these areas it can result in some exhausting hard work and perhaps some wounds along the way, as the first dis-ciples discovered. Nevertheless, for the Christian this journey will always appear as the 'easy way', because for the Christian it is the only way to travel – this easy–hard following of Jesus.

Christianity involves change. I will argue that it involves learning, which is essentially a process of change. That is what makes it hard, for human beings usually find change hard. But the main context of this learning is nothing unusual or extraordinary, but rather our everyday, ever-changing, this-worldly life. And the learning that is required of the Christian is not particularly academic or scholarly, but *spiritual* learning. Like the first disciples, following their teacher on his journey to Jerusalem, we learn Christ best 'on the road'. As they followed, they changed; his road, his 'way' changed them (see Luke 9.51, 57–62; 13.22–25; 14.25–33; Mark 19.1–28).

In our case, this road can only be *our* everyday road, our ordinary way.

Themes

In this book I want to map some of the contours of the pilgrimage of our life, and to discuss the gradients, bends and cambers of that road as occasions of spiritual vision. It is here that we may come to encounter the Christ of the everyday, and learn to forge an ordinary spirituality for our own lives.

In the first chapter of the book I focus on the significance for spiritual living of our day-to-day experience, relating this to the idea of 'spiritual vision' and the learning that discipleship involves. In Chapter 2 I develop this metaphor of vision in terms of seeing things in religious or spiritual depth, and caution against the danger of superficiality in religion.

In the chapters that follow I move from form to content. Chapters 3 and 4 explore two of the most significant of human experiences – our sense of aloneness or isolation, and our experience of friendship. I argue that we should face what these experiences teach us about ourselves and about whatever we take to be our God. I then try to be both honest and positive about what most people agree is the most severe challenge to faith, and to any sense of meaning in our lives: the apparently pointless experience of human suffering and loss. In Chapter 6 I attempt to trace a connection between this experience and the transforming power of a very different emotion (and perception) that is also part and parcel of everyday living – joy.

The final chapters return to the motifs of vision and depth. In Chapter 7 I examine the relationship between superficiality and depth in our everyday stories and the Christian story, and in our social and religious life; and suggest how their *end* or goal may share in some form of resurrection. In the final chapter I apply the themes of discipleship-learning and vision to our perception of Jesus, who calls us to the Christian Way, and argue that even here our spiritual vision tells us a great deal about ourselves by revealing the values that drive our everyday living.

Audience and approach

I have written in as non-technical a way as possible, addressing myself mainly to Christians who are not particularly concerned with the technicalities of theology. I hope that this material will strike a chord for others as well, including those non-Christians who are still willing to listen to what Christians say about life and faith, provided that it is neither too naïve nor too strident. At the other end of the spectrum, some clergy and students of theology may also find something worth reading here – if only to disagree with it!

Like Christianity itself, this book is both simple and hard. I believe that all forms of Christian communication should have as their ultimate aim the intention to arouse, deepen and strengthen faith. This is a simple objective. But this faith must always be an authentic faith, and in the end it will have to be an adult faith. It should always therefore strive for an honesty-to-the-way-you-see-things, and that can be hard. Naturally, I want others to see things as I do. But I have been around long enough to know that many disagree with much that I hold most dear. That's life, so I have to accept it; especially as bashing people on the head with clever arguments and 'self-evident truths' rarely works anyway. Religious and spiritual discussion needs something gentler and more realistic.

Not that we should ever give up on arguments. Although I am the first to claim that reason is not at the heart of religion, in the sense of its deepest motivation and foundation, this does not mean that it can be cavalierly sidelined. Hard thinking must always be a central strand of adult faith, as it is central to being an adult. But the hard thinking that I take a stab at in this book is not, I hope, too abstract or esoteric. It is, rather, an attempt at *depth*, which is something in principle open to all and addresses the debates that all thinking Christians are already engaged in within themselves, at least at some level. For this reason, I haven't shrunk from quoting some rather radical Christian thinkers, as well as facing some challenging criticisms of Christianity. Those who refuse to listen to such 'heresies' tend to end up with a faith that is very often – and very obviously – much the poorer for it, not just intellectually but spiritually. We need to be more open-minded than that; and I have tried to be as open as I can in this book.

The deeper thinking I wish to recognize and encourage as an authentic expression of contemporary Christian living must be personal. Outside the academic fold, faith is a personal reaction in

which we can speak only for ourselves. This should not to be regarded with either shame or contempt, for it is the mark of genuine
religion. Any serious account of everyday life from a Christian
perspective has to be personal. My institute is currently engaged in
researching what we call 'ordinary theology' – that is, the religious
beliefs of those who have not studied religion in any academic or
scholarly way. In interviewing people who describe themselves and
their beliefs as 'just ordinary', we find that they often refer to particular life experiences, relationships and events as the key factors
that have changed their religious beliefs, whether by deepening and
strengthening them, or by eroding them. Their insights and convic-
tions are not second-hand things which they only know about from
books and lectures. They represent a personal framework of life
and faith. In spiritual matters, we must *all* be willing to speak for
ourselves and acknowledge the real influences on our fundamental
beliefs and values.

I have not hidden the personal dimension of my own faith here.
I hope, therefore, that you will forgive a certain amount of personal
anecdote in what follows, as I attempt to do some 'anecdotal theology' myself. In responding to an author's accent, readers are sometimes encouraged to find their own voice.

No big deal

Our theological, religious and spiritual assertions should be expressed quite cautiously. And the more personal and anecdotal our
theology, the more tentative we should be. I confess at the outset that
all I have to offer is a part of what is a much greater whole ('spirituality', 'faith', 'Christ'); and that it is, inevitably, a fairly personal part,
since it is *my* part. I won't pretend that these emphases and dimensions cover everything that is of importance in the spiritual life. This
stuff is not all the stuff that there ought to be; but, at least for me, it
is a very significant part of that everything. (Even for me, this isn't
all there is to my faith. Unfortunately, however, on reading a book

entitled *My Favourite Blue Things*, we tend to think, 'Doesn't he like anything red?')

None of this is particularly original, either. Others think similarly and have written similarly, as the wide range of quotations I shall use reveals. I suspect that you have had many of these thoughts yourself. Indeed, I hope so, for I want to argue that the best religious books are those that tell their readers what they already know.

So there we are. I can only say what I can say, and leave it to others to say the rest. After all, my main theme is that we can only have our own faith, as we tread our own journey and learn in our own way.

And with that double entendre (or is it just a pun?), it is time to set off . . .

1

On learning Christ in the ordinary way

———•◆•———

Ordinariness is our indispensable anchorage: without it we are nothing and nowhere . . . This perception of the religious weight of ordinariness can deliver people from the tyranny of various sorts of spiritual elitism . . .

Don Cupitt

What's so wrong with being ordinary?

Much religion, spirituality and theology concentrates, very properly, on the extraordinary. We are encouraged to contemplate the lives of 'out of the ordinary' heroes and heroines of the faith, and to reflect on claims to unique revelations and 'acts of God'. We are prompted to engage in religious activities – prayer, worship and spiritual exercises – that are very different from, and are often designed to take us away from, our everyday lives. Some religious pundits would also invite us to seek out, or lay ourselves open to, religious experiences that are well beyond the routine.

But most of the time most of us focus on the *everyday*, the *ordinary*; at least most of me does. And, again, 'very properly' so. Perhaps more so . . .

I once witnessed a parish mission led by members of a religious order. They were all nice guys, but from what I saw they spent far too much time talking about their differences from everybody else: in particular, their vows of poverty, chastity and obedience, and how they affected their lives. This might have been all well and good in

1

its place, but it seemed to me that this was not the place for it. Anyway, the retired miners and the busy mothers to whom they spoke were not that impressed; and the handful of sulky adolescents who had been persuaded to come along certainly weren't. 'We want to know', someone said, 'how to be Christians here, in *our* lives.' It was a fair comment. Their Christianity needed to be lived out at their places of work and in their pubs and clubs, or at home and among the drying nappies, with the rent or the mortgage to pay. Or they had to do it at school and on the streets among their friends. They had to deal in very different ways with money and possessions; sex, love and relationships; and a great range of other conflicting concerns of a secular life. 'Isn't the gospel for us as well?' 'Do our vows and our values not matter?'

I'm with them. It's one thing to do the Christian thing on a retreat or in a church. But it's at work on Monday morning or late on Thursday evening, or at home any time when family worries or tensions with the neighbours (or the plumbers) hang heavily upon me, that I really discern the narrowness and steepness – and the power and the point – of the road. Looking across the city from the hillside, the view of the cathedral may be clear and the air pleasant; but if I want to get closer to it I shall have to make my way through the grime and chaos of the back alleys, and across the dangerous traffic of the roads of everyday life. For me, and for most people, there are no short cuts.

There must be some sort of connection, of course, down from the out-of-the-ordinary religious thoughts, practices, beliefs, ways of life and experiences to the terrain of our ordinary lives. But sometimes (again, at least for me) those links often seem strained and unconvincing, and the pathways uninviting, hard to find or even sometimes firmly barred against us. So we stick with the commonplace, with what we know. If we are to think religiously at all, then, we shall need to begin at our end – the ordinary end – and to do our spiritual thinking 'from below'.

That is what I shall attempt here. I want to say something Christian about everyday life, what we may call the *ordinary spiritual life*. I want to articulate the puzzling claim that religious people sometimes make about finding God within their day-to-day lives, 'finding God in the midst'.

Everyday God

On another occasion while I was an ordinand in training, I was informed by a young theologian (now a professor) that what I was doing when I visited the male surgical ward of the local infirmary was 'taking the transcendent God into hospital'. (Meeting all those people with hernias at least got the Deity out of the house, I suppose.) His remark was possibly only an exercise in shock tactics, designed to prevent my thinking that I was training to be an amateur social worker or a nursing auxiliary; but all the same I didn't like it. And I don't like it any more now. A God who can be taken to a place where God is not already present is not God.

The young theologian's pious assertion was, in fact, a form of atheism. There are many types of unbelief, after all, and some of them masquerade as purer forms of religion. One example looks for God *only* in special things: in dramatic miracles, in unexpected answers to prayer, in unforgettable mystical or charismatic experiences, or in the gaps and mysteries that mark the holes in our current scientific explanations. I don't deny that God may be there, but if so it is only because God is already everywhere: in the ordinary things of life, as well as the special things; in creation before, and at the same time as, redemption. If God is not everywhere, God is not anywhere. So if God is not *here*, then there is no God worthy of the name.

However, that claim probably sounds too general and therefore too remote. Life is about the particular. The everyday is, after all, a jumble of particular situations, experiences, responsibilities, demands and people. So let me steal some words from a writer on preaching:

> Of course, God is at work in all things. Of course, the whole of creation is the object of God's love. Of course, Christ was lifted up on the cross to draw all people to himself. But I thought I heard him say, as he was hanging there, 'Take my mother home.'

Spiritual change

In a way, belief in God does not change anything; and yet it changes everything. The philosophical genius, Ludwig Wittgenstein, said of philosophy that when it is done properly it 'leaves everything as it is'. He meant by this that it shouldn't overturn our usual ways of speaking and thinking, but rather make them clearer, allowing us to see everything as it really is – to see the heart and truth of things, grounded in ordinary life and ordinary talk. Good religion and good theology should do something similar.

That is one of the things that is so startling and exciting about Jesus. He brings with him no new theology and no new world, nothing different. But he shows us the old world and the old theology in a new light. This is a large part of what religious people call revelation. So Jesus reveals that – despite appearances – the widow's mite was a giving 'more than all of them' (Luke 21.3), the foreigner is my neighbour (Luke 10.36–37), and tomorrow is another day (Matthew 6.34). In a way, we knew all this before. But we didn't understand it before, not as we do now. *Of course* this is just common bread and wine; of course he is just the carpenter's son; of course this congregation is a bunch of miserable sinners. But they are *also* the body of the Christ, full of grace and truth. And while Christ may be there specially and distinctly, he is not only there. What is true there is true because it is also true here, if perhaps to a lesser extent.

The God who is in all things can reveal his character through all things. The knack is to see it.

We may call this spiritual vision. Spirituality is all about seeing. Spiritual people are nothing particularly special, except that they are able to recognize this, that and the other as God's this, that and the other. They see the remarkable in the mundane. They see Nature, friendship, joy and struggle as 'holy things' – things that express God's rule, hand and intention. They have learned to spot the Kingdom, the realm of God, as it grows secretly like a mustard seed or looms large and urgent outside the gates. They may have few other advantages, few worldly gifts and little status, but they are spiritually blessed – for to be able to see the 'signs of the Kingdom' is to be a sign of the Kingdom oneself.

Not surprisingly, vision is a key word throughout religion. I think of this vision as a new take on what has always been before us. A more vocal group will only use the word to denote rare, gut-wrenchingly awesome, charismatic or mystical (or even visionary) experiences – dramatic and explicit 'religious experiences' of the transcendent. Such a stance makes good sense to those who have had these encounters, but they (and we) should not pretend that such extraordinary experiences are bestowed on everyone. And even when this sort of vision is given to people, in order for it to be of any lasting value it has got to lead to a different type of *envisioning* that may be applied to everything. It must have an effect on the way people see things generally, on their ordinary view of ordinary things. It must result in a *re*vision of everyday experience.

To be converted is, in the end, not so much a matter of seeing different things, as of seeing the same things differently. It involves seeing this child, woman or man – or this slice of the natural world or sliver of historical time – *as* holy, as sacred, as God's. Seeing life as a spiritual journey is not really about seeing something else, something *additional*.

My most vivid dream ever involved being out at night on a hillside and suddenly seeing among the stars an enormous, brilliantly lit, stained-glass window, its apex towering up above me. I awoke terrified. I trace this back to an occasion in the London Planetarium as a child, when the dome with its virtual stars was suddenly illuminated with huge images based on the traditional names of the constellations.

Needless to say, perhaps, I have never had such an experience while awake, although I have often been struck with awe and wonder on a cold moorland away from the city lights, when the stars seemed without number and our galaxy's 'Milky Way' stood out as a ribbon of diffuse light spilling across the sky. Awesome indeed and a spiritual experience, but one in which I saw nothing 'additional' to the natural phenomena that labelled their significance.

If faith is not based on some additional experience, something added to our day-to-day experience, we must think about it in terms of seeing more clearly and in more depth something that is already and always there. Something like the meaning of life or the hand of God. This is what it is like to see through the eyes of faith. And to have the eyes of faith is the most important component of being a person of faith. In the spiritual realm, when people talk about what they experience, they are not only talking about the nature of some 'outer' reality. They are also speaking about themselves.

We might develop an analogy here. I need to be in the right place geographically (or astronomically) even to see the Milky Way, although it is always there. Similarly, I need to be 'in the right place' spiritually in order to see the point of my life. 'Success' here (unfortunately) is as much about me as it is about what there is to be seen. To be able to see the Kingdom of God, I need already to be a part of it. The eccentric English poet and visionary William Blake wrote, in the less gender-free language of the eighteenth century, 'As a man is, so he sees. As the eye is formed, such are its powers.' A gloomier Danish writer of the following century (Søren Kierkegaard) expressed a very similar view:

> The crucial thing is what the observer himself is . . . When evil dwells in the heart then the eye sees evil, but when purity abides in the heart then the eye sees the finger of God; for the pure always see God . . . what is in a man, then, decides what he discovers and what he conceals.

This is about me, then; for it all depends who we are. To see things differently, therefore, we may have to change. But don't think that this 'purity of heart' is about unspotted, external moral cleanliness. That is one of the many big mistakes that people make about religion. Religion is particularly open to misunderstanding – not least by its adherents, as we shall see. And one of the biggest mistakes that people both inside and outside the Church make about Christianity is that it is reserved 'for the righteous'. The Christian gospel declares exactly the opposite. The purity that Jesus calls for lies much deeper than morality, and very much deeper than our superficial moral judgements about one another. Neither pure hands nor pure thoughts are its precondition, but a pure heart. And that means an *open* heart – one that is open to the world, to other people and ultimately to God. One that is really, deep-down open. The Church, wrote Karl Barth, is only holy 'in its openness'.

Learning Christ

So much for the word 'ordinary' in the title of this chapter. But what about that curious phrase, 'learning Christ'?

First of all, let me apologize to any readers for whom the word 'learning' conjures up grim times at school or college, when their own concerns were ignored and their sense of self-worth eroded. 'Education' can do that; we can suffer an education without learning much that is either wholesome or life-giving. Nevertheless, even if we bunk off school we can never avoid learning – for most of our learning happens before, after and outside educational institutions. Life teaches us. Inevitably, we are learning all the time.

But are we 'learning Christ'? This may seem an odd form of words to use, if only because it is so close to 'learning *about* Christ'. Learning about Christ is a much less contentious matter. That phrase marks a scholarly, educational exercise that any one can engage in, whether they have a Christian commitment or not. 'Learning Christ' is different. It is not incompatible with such scholarship, and learning Christ is a valid method of learning about him. But learning Christ is much more than 'Christian studies' or 'the quest of the historical Jesus'. Learning Christ is the obedient learning of the *disciple*.

Anecdote 54 (I've already lost count): Some years ago I worked as a tutor for a course for senior police officers. (Don't ask – I suppose I was just in the wrong place at the wrong time.) The tutors' task was to help the groups discuss a topic. My group's topic was 'discipline'. Sensibly, its members ignored most of my comments until I pointed out that the word 'discipline' didn't just mean 'order, rules and control', but also mental and moral learning. I added that the word originated in the Latin for 'disciple'.

I soon learned what it's like to be fitted up by the police. Each group had to give a presentation to the whole conference, the text of which we prepared together. But my students had their own ideas about the manner in which this should be presented, and they didn't seek my advice. So that is how, one fateful night, I was invited to take the vacant chair set at a long table, while the would-be chief superintendents sat down, six on each side of me, to present their thoughts on the meaning of discipline. They concluded their presentation by bringing out bread and wine and passing it to me . . .

The Christian apprentice

All learning is change, and Christian learning is the change in attitudes, beliefs and dispositions wrought through the process of becoming a disciple, and continuing as a disciple. In New Testament Greek the disciple is the *mathetes*, the 'one who directs his mind'. Significantly, it is a term used of the apprentice. To learn in this way is very different from any distanced and dispassionate 'learning about' something, or even someone. It is a form of learning that originated well outside any school or college.

Apprentices are thinner on the ground than they used to be, even if they now sometimes appear on TV. But spending time as an apprentice was, and in some places still is, the only way to learn the practical skills of a trade. It was a distinction that a man had 'served his time' as the phrase was, at least on the lips of my cabinet-maker father. (When I was little I was puzzled that he was so proud of having been to prison!) Apprenticeship takes time. During this time, apprentices learn more than skills. They also learn the trade's attendant traditions – including its language, its duties and responsibilities, and its appropriate character virtues and demeanour. You learn not only to act like your mentor–master acts, with the saw and plane. You also learn – to an extent – to be as he is. In modelling yourself on your teacher, you come to see the wood, the joints and the whole craft-practice as he sees them. You are formed with and in his vision. 'Following in the master's way' is a very wide-ranging form of learning.

'That is not the way you learned Christ', the author of the letter to the Ephesians once wrote. What he was referring to was the sort of spiritual *mis*understanding that results in ignorance, hardness of heart, lack of sensitivity and indulgence. He did not believe that these could be the outcomes of 'learning Christ'. Yet, surely, they had been 'taught in him, as truth is in Jesus' (Ephesians 4.20–21). The true learning of Christ – and here the text uses a word that is similar to the word for disciple – involves directing one's mind towards him. One New Testament scholar has described this as learning the truth 'in the authentic Jesus-way'.

We may think of it as *discipleship learning*. Jesus' disciples were not student–learners so much as 'apprentice–learners'. As we have seen, such learning is personal and experiential – 'hands-on', in fact. The disciples, too, are granted fellowship and a share in the master's life and course; they are 'stamped and fashioned' by their teacher, and may be called to serve as a witness to him. Like the apprentice cabinet-maker, the disciples' work was 'not study but practice'; their teacher was 'the master-craftsman whom they were to follow and imitate'. So Jesus is 'the master, not just of texts and sayings but of the practices that are learned, not so much by reading about them, but by engaging in them'.

Engagement. Practice. Hands-on experience. Discipleship learning requires undertaking things as well as hearing them. So it is no surprise that learning Christ is essentially learning *on the way*. Jesus teaches his disciples as they follow him along the road – whether that be the road of the first disciples, travelling to and from the Jerusalem of the final conflict and the new beginning, or through our more routine progressions.

What are the features of this apprenticeship learning? In the following chapters I will explore some of its more significant characteristics by considering concrete examples of everyday spiritual learning. But perhaps I might mention two aspects now.

The first concerns the vulnerability of the learner. The disciples leave their nets, and their other trades and skills, in order to follow Jesus. They also leave the protection of their homes, families and friends. Soon – far too soon, it must have seemed – he sends them out to speak of what they have learned on the road. 'We learn by going and teach by sending,' writes Craig Dykstra.

> We come to know new things, feel in new ways, do things differently when we find ourselves in a new place . . . [I]n new situations the habits are disturbed, the routines upset, and the filters readjusted. We become vulnerable to being changed.
>
> To be sent is to become vulnerable. Vulnerability is the key to education.

Our roads take us along a terrain that is both old and new. Like war, life consists of long periods of boredom interspersed with moments of terror. Much is familiar, but any new twist of the road can open us to the shock of the new. It must be so, if we are truly to learn. Let us hope that whatever lies around the corner will treat us gently.

Many children hate school because they feel vulnerable there, away from the comfortable support of family – and perhaps of friends too – and challenged to learn hard skills and understand difficult ideas. In order to learn, adults also need to be open to the changes of learning and the wounds of experience, and most of us don't like it much. I shouldn't speak for others, but I know how hard it is for me to see things clearly, and how painful it can be when my attitudes and beliefs change. So be gentle with me, if that is what you intend. I suppose some people are converted by being shouted at or made to feel a fool before their peers – but not many. Jesus was not always gentle with his disciples, but he was a much more lenient teacher than many of his successors. Religion is not best taught by ranters, nor spirituality by the severe. The road is going to be hard enough for most of us and necessarily so; there is no need to make it worse.

There is a kindness that is proper to teaching the way of the cross.

Revision notes

The second feature of our discipleship learning that I want to discuss here picks up again that metaphor of sight. Spiritual learning, I believe, is essentially ophthalmic; it is a correction of vision. 'Now can you read the bottom line?' Or, as my optician put it when he presented me with my first pair of spectacles, 'You didn't realize the world looked like that, did you?'

The biblical story is about seeing, and it is about choosing. It is about seeing the light shining in the darkness and moving towards it. What is needed for both, very often, is a change of view. And that is precisely what is on offer from the Christian gospel: a new way of seeing, a restructuring of sight. I believe that all the processes of Church – its organization, fellowship, worship, outreach, pastoral and prophetic ministry – all of these should serve the fundamental purpose of the formation, purification and redirection of our vision, so that we may see more clearly and choose with open eyes.

The New Testament gives us the story of those who saw a Mediterranean peasant healing and preaching, and left everything to follow him. We may think of their journey as a pilgrimage of seeing, for Christian vision and discipleship are about seeing things for what they really are and then choosing them. That is what it means to recognize the Kingdom of God, and to worship only that which is worthy of worship. 'Open your eyes, for God's sake', Jesus seems to be telling us. 'And see properly.' This is the vision that necessitates our re-vision of everything. Nothing can remain untouched; for the kingdoms of this world must become the Kingdom of our Lord and of his Christ.

It includes seeing *the point of things*. More venerable readers may recall a Monty Python sketch in which a merchant banker (John Cleese,

I think) was negotiating with a charity collector, selling paper flags in aid of orphans. The banker is deeply puzzled: 'I don't follow this at all . . . it looks to me as though I'm a pound down on the whole deal.' In matters of religion, too, it is very easy to miss the point. We can read the texts, engage in the practices, maybe even work up some enthusiasm for it all – only to miss the point entirely. We can learn all about the rich variety of trees in the forest, and remain wholly ignorant of the nature of wood. As with jokes, sometimes we just can't get it.

Much of Jesus' teaching was confrontational. But he didn't seem to take on the sinners, the traditional enemies of God and religion. Instead, he seems to have confronted the friends of faith. The Pharisees, in particular, or at least some of them, got it in the neck. He called them snakes, a 'brood of vipers' (Matthew 12.34), which is not the language one would expect to be addressed to those who kept strictly to God's commandments and earnestly hoped for the coming of God's Kingdom. But in Jesus' eyes, many of them had simply missed the point. They knew it all, did it all, hoped for and believed in it all – and got it all wrong. So badly wrong, in fact, that their diet of religious and moral purity involved filtering out midges while gulping down camels (Matthew 23.24). So badly wrong, that they ended up condemning Jesus' healings as the work of the Devil (Matthew 12.24).

Those who missed the point gave themselves away by making their religion a mark of honour in the synagogues and respect in the marketplace, taking a pride in it before others and even before God (Matthew 23.5–7). According to Luke (18.9–14), Jesus once told a parable 'to some who trusted in themselves that they were righteous and regarded others with contempt'. In this story, a Pharisee thanks God for his own piety and morality; and especially that he is not like that tax collector in the back pew. This was natural, for tax collectors were almost by definition rogues and thieves – quisling-Jews working for the occupying Roman powers and cheating to line their own pockets.

But in Jesus' story, the tax collector is praying too, lowering his eyes and muttering, 'God, be merciful to me, a sinner.' And the point? 'All who exalt themselves will be humbled, but all who humble themselves will be exalted.'

This theme lies at the heart of Christianity; it is a great part of the point of it. If we don't get this, what on earth shall we make of the rest of it? Paul offers his own interpretation in what might once have been an ancient Christian hymn. It is a hymn about Christ . . .

> who, though he was in the form of God,
>> did not regard equality with God
>> as something to be grasped [possibly the word is 'exploited'],
> but emptied himself,
>> taking the form of a slave . . .
>> he humbled himself
>> and became obedient to the point of death –
>> even death on a cross.

(Philippians 2.6–8)

The remainder of the hymn is about God's exalting of this humble servant, so that he receives the highest of names and the worship of all. But to concentrate on that would again be to miss the point. For the point lies in the humbling, the giving up, the becoming a servant to us and for our sakes. This is not to be interpreted as a wily career move, a bit of menial experience to put on the CV or the university application form. It is not Jesus' way of catching the boss's eye so that he may be promoted to higher things – to *true* greatness – leaving the rest of us behind on the shop floor. Most of us have seen, and maybe even sometimes engaged in, these forms of pretend humility. *This*, however, is the real thing. It is the recognition that the way of self-giving service is the only sort of greatness in God's eyes. To see the point of Jesus is to begin to see through those eyes.

The point is that equality with God is not about grabbing, grasping and holding on to status and power; exploiting them for our own glory. Rather, God is found in the letting go – 'in taking the form of a slave', in washing the feet of the unworthy.

This is the wood from which the trees are made. This is the point of Jesus and this is the deep essence of God. So this is what we are to learn in learning Christ, and this is how we are to learn him.

In short, therefore, 'learning Christ in the ordinary way' is a question of learning the true meaning of Christ, and of learning other things 'in the way of Jesus'; and of doing all this in and from our normal, everyday, workaday, day-by-day life. This 'Christly learning' is also 'godly learning', because to learn Christ on the road is to discover the truth of the gospel and of the Christ-like God.

2

The deeper gospel

Then they sent to him some Pharisees and some Herodians to trap him in what he said. And they came and said to him, 'Teacher, we know that you are sincere, and show deference to no one; for you do not regard people with partiality, but teach the way of God in accordance with truth. Is it lawful to pay taxes to the emperor, or not? Should we pay them, or should we not?' But knowing their hypocrisy, he said to them, 'Why are you putting me to the test? Bring me a denarius and let me see it.' And they brought one. Then he said to them, 'Whose head is this, and whose title?' They answered, 'The emperor's.' Jesus said to them, 'Give to the emperor the things that are the emperor's, and to God the things that are God's.' And they were utterly amazed at him.

Mark 12.13–17

Looking at the face

Like much of the Christian gospel, this familiar text speaks about surfaces and about depths. It concerns faces and what lies beneath them.

The face of Tiberius Caesar Augustus is inscribed on the surface of the coin that Jesus asks his enemies to display (proving that they, at any rate, are part of the Roman order that they so much hate). Whatever else it is, the face of the emperor is an image of worldly power and success. Caesar will have his way in this world and must be paid his dues. But Jesus insists that our fuller, more radical and more comprehensive duty lies deeper. It is the obligation to acknowledge, and to respond to, that which belongs to God.

The answer of the coin is Jesus' response to a trap. It has been set with a little flattery: 'Teacher, we know that you . . . show deference to no one.' In the Revised Standard Version translation of 1946 this reads, 'You do not regard the position of men.' The original Greek translates literally, 'You do not look at the face of men . . . [but on the truth that the way of God teaches].'

'You do not look at the face . . .' The Old Testament uses similar phrases in the context of showing partiality towards others, and being unduly influenced by them. The meaning here is that Jesus does not 'regard people with partiality'. It is in this sense that Jesus does not look at faces.

Plumbing the depths

Religion is about depth. As such it sees beyond the surface and the presentation, behind 'the face'. This is not just because religion is mysterious, hidden or obscure; although, we should admit, a great deal of it often is. To make the claim that religion is about depth is certainly not the same as saying that religion should ignore or disparage the surface, if by the surface we mean the everyday world and our everyday life. On the contrary, the Bible is all about the everyday – its work and play; its pain and death; its hope, joy and sex. But religion is concerned with finding a depth in and through the everyday.

We might try a metaphor here. It is as if, looking at a particular object from above, I know only that it is 'round' and 'brown', 'wooden' and 'shiny'. It could be any round piece of wood – attractively figured and polished, possibly, but ultimately fairly useless. This appears to be its 'face value': its apparent nature, what it is 'on the face of it'. But if I view the same object from the side I will see that it has depth or height, a third dimension to add to the other two. Perceiving this, I know now that it is something more useful, for there is a lot more to it. After all, a round piece of wood is just, well, a round piece of wood. But with legs underneath it is a round *table* – and we know how valuable that can be, if we want to start discussing the quest for the Holy Grail, or solving a political dispute, or inviting both sets of in-laws to tea at the same time.

Religion claims to be about depth. It speaks of a power and a love below things that keeps everything up and running. This is an affirmation that is both about fact and about feeling, a confession that is both cosmological and psychological (and therefore spiritual). Religion is not only an insight into the foundations of the world, but one that also speaks of the anchoring points of life and the river beds of human meaning.

Jesus sees such depths in things and – particularly – in people. So he does not judge by appearances, as God does not (1 Samuel 16.7; John 7.24; 2 Corinthians 5.12). He is not superficial; he is not shallow. He does not 'look at the face of men'.

Which is, of course, all very well for him. Fair enough, if that is the sort of guy he is. The drawback is that he challenges us to do the same. He insists that we should not stick with face values, either, but look for the depth in people and in situations. We are goaded by his words to see the complexity and the value of people and things, unveiling features that usually lie deep below the surface.

This form of spiritual, moral and religious seeing can be very difficult. For many it does not come naturally at all, and popular culture sets no great store by it. It has, by the way, nothing much to do with being *clever*; or at least not with being intellectually clever. Indeed many intellectually clever people (including some academic theologians) are quite bad at it and quite stupid about it, often missing the deep currents as they chase the fascinating surface reflections on the water. Possibly it does have something to do with what people now call 'interpersonal intelligence', 'emotional intelligence' or even 'spiritual intelligence'. Although it does not seem to be a developmental thing, it is related to being *mature* in that we can learn the skill – the knack – of this seeing, given time. For it does take time, because we can learn it only by seeing a lot of things and, especially, by listening a lot to people. Maybe even 'mature' isn't the right word, then. A better word might be *wise*.

Apparently, the words 'wise' and 'wisdom' derive from a root that means 'to see'. Wisdom is a form of vision, then. To be able to see into the depths is to have spiritual wisdom.

Fathoming fame

I want to touch on certain aspects of life where this wisdom of depth is highly significant, even though contemporary society resists it. That resistance is a consequence of our quick-fix, 'solve-your-problems-with-a-makeover', 'be-sure-your-face-fits' culture. Not infrequently, I fear, the Church itself reflects such superficial values.

Take the examples of fame and status. Too often, fame is just face stuff, surface stuff. We have all heard or read interviews with young men and women whose deepest ambition is that they desperately want one thing above all else, 'to be famous'. So they also want to be a quiz show host, or a TV weather girl, or – I don't know – the person who assassinates the Teletubbies. It wouldn't matter much what they become in the end, because they don't really want to be famous *for* anything – for doing anything, for being anyone. They just want to be 'in the limelight'. They don't want to be celebrated for their knowledge, skill or wit; not even for their beautiful bodies. They just want to be, as the saying goes, famous for being famous.

And why not? Lots of people want fame. And a few actually have it. But the trouble is that fame often diminishes their lives. The famous may enjoy their fame provided that they can escape from it whenever they want to, so that they can 'be themselves'. Mostly, however, they can't. So we often hear, 'It would be wrong to say he resisted fame . . . The problem was, of course, that fans would not let him be a normal person.'

But that's not really our problem. Our problem, as the non-famous, is that the fame of the famous tends to demean us. Despite Andy Warhol, not everyone *could* be world famous for 15 minutes –

not even just for two minutes. Fame only works if just a few people have it. The very existence of fame depends on the rest of us serving as voyeurs of the famous, a situation that can result in our being more interested in the superficial veneer of a few strangers than we are in our own families or friends, not to mention the rest of the human race – or even ourselves.

Fame must be selective. The same could be said of status, since there can be no high status for some without there being many others who are comparatively more lowly. And lowliness can hurt. This is not a 'classist' moan, fuelled by left-wing ideology or simple old-fashioned envy. It is a fact that high-status people can do the rest of us harm even when they don't intend it. The clinical psychologist Oliver James draws on social comparison theory to explain much of the depression that is widespread in our society. He lays some of the blame on the mass media for encouraging 'undiscounted upward comparison', and concludes, 'There is little doubt that American film and television are hugely destructive to our well-being.' All those beautiful, wealthy and successful people just make us feel terrible; they make us feel we are 'losers'. Alain de Botton defines 'status anxiety' as:

> a worry, so pernicious as to be capable of ruining extended stretches of our lives, that we are in danger of failing to conform to the ideals of success laid down by our society and that we may as a result be stripped of dignity and respect.

De Botton insists that we can fight this anxiety; and among the resources available for combating it he lists Christianity, including its 'sense of the preciousness of every human being'.

I wish those young men and women well in their quest for fame, as I do the many others who desire status above all things. They are welcome to it. But let us pursue instead a search for the wisdom of depth, because superficiality is very bad news for most people, and it should be anathema to religion and the Church. We need to go beyond it.

In one of his poems, Rudyard Kipling muses about a heaven for painters after the death of their critics. He writes that in this realm 'only The Master shall praise us, and only The Master shall blame':

> And no one shall work for money, and no one shall work for fame,
> But each for the joy of the working, and each, in his separate star,
> Shall draw the Thing as he sees It for the God of Things as
> They are!

'The God of Things as They are' is not seduced or fooled, as we so often are, by superficialities.

Concerning others

I want to focus on three areas in which superficiality can poison our understanding and relationships. I will attempt to say something first about others, then about the Christian gospel and finally about God. Let's take other people first (which is not a bad motto in itself).

For Jesus, Mary Magdalene was 'Mary' (John 20.16). She was not a whore, an adulterer, a breaker-up of families, a 'disturbed person' – although she may have been any or all of these things, even ignoring Dan Brown's recent speculations. 'Mary'. And Zacchaeus was 'Zacchaeus'. For Jesus, he was not a runty stunted crook, a quisling working for the enemy, a rich cheat. When Jesus saw him up a tree seeking a better view, he looked up and said, 'Zacchaeus, hurry and come down; for I must stay at your house today' (Luke 19.5).

This was a significant part of the scandal of Jesus. (The New Testament is very clear that Jesus frequently scandalized people – his family and friends, as well as his enemies.) To Jesus the blind weren't just blind men, and the mad weren't just mad women, and sinners were never just sinners. They were all people: children of God – whole, valuable *persons*. So he spoke and ate with them; he taught them and healed them. And he forgave them.

Again, we might respond that this is all very well for him. But the words and actions of Jesus are never just about Jesus. They interrogate and challenge our lives also. 'The one who believes in me will also do the works that I do and, in fact, will do greater works than these,' Jesus promises, in those anxiety-inducing words from John 14.12. No story about Jesus is simply about Jesus and not also about us.

Implicitly, therefore, we are being instructed here not to judge superficially. We are not to stereotype or dismiss the young as just young; nor the old as just old; nor the enemy, the asylum-seeker or the foreigner, the servant or master, the woman or man, gay or straight, poor or rich as *only* that. We are called to recognize them as persons, all depth under the face . . .

The worst sin is to view people so superficially that we do not see them as persons at all, but merely as objects to use. In our relationships at the checkout till or with the telephone call centre, the temptation to treat people as objects is almost irresistible, partly because we think that the businesses that employ them perceive them like that themselves, and partly because we sense that that is how those businesses also view us – as commodities to be converted into profit. The Jewish religious philosopher, Martin Buber, wrote eloquently about the importance of relating to the other through participation, mutuality, empathy and encounter: as a 'Thou' to be met, rather than – in abstraction and separation – as an 'It' to be used. 'When *Thou* is spoken, the speaker has no thing for his object . . . If I face a human being as my *Thou*, and say the primary word *I-Thou* to him, he is not a thing among things, and does not consist of things.' Buber adds, 'Every particular *Thou* is a glimpse through to the eternal *Thou*.'

No human act is more superficial than treating another person as an object to be manipulated for our own good, a means to our ends, and not as someone of intrinsic value who is an end in himself or herself. In Terry Pratchett's Discworld, even the witch Granny Weatherwax knows that; and she insists on this truth against the unimpressive priest of Om, one 'Mightily Oats', who is suspicious of such an ordinary theology. Here Granny has asked what the Omnian holy men discuss.

'There is a very interesting debate raging at the moment about the nature of sin . . .'

'And what do they think? Against it, are they?'

'It's not as simple as that. It's not a black and white issue. There are so many shades of grey.'

'Nope.'

'Pardon?'

'There's no greys, only white that's got grubby. I'm surprised you don't know that. And sin, young man, is when you treat people as things. Including yourself. That's what sin is.'

'It's a lot more complicated than that –'

'No. It ain't. When people say things are a lot more complicated than that, they means they're getting worried that they won't like the truth. People as things, that's where it starts.'

'Oh, I'm sure there are worse crimes –'

'But they *starts* with thinking about people as things . . .'

It is sometimes said, when someone falls under the wheels of the juggernaut of psychological illness, or a marriage breaks up, or a friend or a stranger (particularly a famous stranger) is caught out in a foolishness or a sin, 'Who would have believed it?' That too is superficial talk, and shows only a superficial understanding. We should know better than that. We should know that we don't know what goes on in most people's lives; that we are almost wholly ignorant of their problems, their battles and their despairs. Nor do we usually know their hidden corners of courage, faithfulness or pure goodness. In the face of the disasters of other people, we should not be ashamed of the cliché, 'There but for the grace of God . . .' This is a humbling truth. Even when we serve as the butt of their sin, we need to recall that 'judgement is mine, says the Lord'. That is surely the best place to locate it.

The claim is sometimes made that the true saints are unknown. It could be so. If sanctity is to be measured, at least in part, by our striving to be holy rather than by our achieving holiness, then the mass-murderer who struggles energetically but ineffectively against his dark and destructive inner desires and outer influences may be less culpable and more worthy than the 'natural-born saint' who has never needed to counteract any evil desires in his heart, or many evil influences in his life. Only a God *could* adequately judge such internal moral strivings, which will only ever be partially reflected in a person's outer behaviour. Maybe some tetchy sinners enter the Kingdom of such a God in advance of the sweet-natured, naturally virtuous authors of abundant good works. Being a 'nice person' may not rank quite so high in the eyes of a God who sees inside us. Not if that God knows that some are born good and others achieve goodness easily, but that there are also those who struggle hard and long against the overwhelming odds of their nature and nurture and have little to show for it at the end. We may guess who the 'constitutional Christians' are. But we should not expect to know who is in the group of struggling saints, and that lack of recognition is likely to make their struggle for sanctity even more difficult.

In our thinking and in our lives, then, let us not be superficial about people.

Concerning the gospel

And let us not be superficial about the gospel. Some years ago I was a member of a church discussion group studying Luke's account of the announcement to Mary of her portentous pregnancy (Luke 1.26–38). We were reflecting on what this story of the 'annunciation' might mean for us today, with or without its angelic trimmings. What if we were to say, with Mary, 'Let it be with me according to your word'? How would we face the challenge of allowing Christ to be born in us? I recall that we talked in some depth about what such obedience to the will of God might imply for our relationships and our lives, our careers and worlds, and our Church.

Then the vicar dropped by and offered *his* interpretation. 'What this text means is that this parish needs a Stewardship Campaign, and that we shall all have to pledge more giving.' Everyone fell silent. I doubt that I was alone in thinking, 'Please do not rob us of the depth of the gospel.'

The Church is too superficial too often. It cares overmuch about its surfaces – about itself and its surfaces. It is a housewifely Martha, whisking off the dust before anyone notices, and hard at work with the polish until the visitors can no longer see any scratches. Martha is the Church's heroine. But, surprisingly, Mary is the one who is commended by its Lord for looking and listening, and seeing and hearing, in depth (Luke 10.38–41).

In their research on why people lapse from church attendance, Philip Richter and Leslie Francis reported the views of one Anglican ex-churchgoer who denounced as 'horrible' her church's 'collective attempt to domesticate the spirit'. 'In her experience, church going was less about the mystery of God and more to do with "people turning and telling you not to sit in that pew because that's where the Brownies sit!" '

The Christian gospel is not superficial news. It is not about superficial things. It is not about worldly power or fame, or any other kind of worldly status (not even for Brownies). Indeed, it stands for the overturning of all such values. The Christian gospel is the good news of the crucifixion of the values of a superficial world. It should not surprise us, therefore, that it sees the poor, the outcast and the old, in the person of the widow at the Temple collection box, as those who give the most, as the last who are really first. And it should not offend us that it celebrates the silent, hidden, unknown goodness of a life of self-giving that seeks no reward and is not done for show.

We need to face the full implications of the unpalatable truth that there are no MBEs or KCBs in the Kingdom of God. And there are no ecclesiastical or academic titles there either; nor are there riches or fame, or any other masks to hide behind. In the Kingdom there is only worship, and giving ourselves up to the will of God. This is the non-ideological, non-political egalitarianism of the Christian gospel. On our knees we are all much closer to the same height.

Jesus' chosen disciples never did get the hang of this; they were, after all, a fairly superficial crew. 'The apostles are not so much evil as thick,' writes William C. Spohn. They just don't get it. 'It is because we have no bread,' they whimper as Jesus condemns the yeast of the Pharisees (Mark 8.16). They even ask whether they may please sit close to Jesus in heaven, when he has only just finished speaking about the necessity of his dying for them on earth, abandoned and friendless. The apostles are simply deplorable. Hopeless.

But we may yet find hope in them, for the dimness and sinfulness of the biblical saints is actually a great comfort. They show us how patient God is with our human superficiality; they show us there is hope for any one of us. This does not make the disciples any the less spiritually superficial. It is just that, as Spohn writes, 'These accounts are mirrors held up for future generations because we can recognize ourselves in the disciples' attitudes and questions. Clearly, we are all "successors to the apostles".' Unfortunately.

Concerning God

And so, finally, to God. Inevitably, we can speak of the mystery of God only in symbols, and God is as well symbolized by the language of depth as by that of height. Obviously, this too is picture language, for God is literally no more 'deep down' than 'far off'. But God is a God of depths, in the sense that God knows us in our depths. (A God who did not would not be God, just as we would not be us without our depths.) It is only a trivial and superficial, and therefore false, religion that pictures God as concerned with the social, moral or religious superficialities, who makes on-the-face-of-things judgements about us. True religion declares to us a God who does not stay on the surface, and is never going to be duped by superficial things.

A God of depths demands yet more of us: not just that we should not assess others on the surface, but that we should not judge God in a perfunctory way either. Embracing a deeper theology ought to suggest to us that we should not round on God quite so quickly when things get hard, as though we did not expect them ever to be hard, and had never noticed that they were sometimes really rather hard for other people. Even God deserves a little more understanding than that, a little more depth of appreciation.

It is good to remember that we know so little about people; it helps us to judge them less superficially. We know even less about God. It may be that God should also sometimes be exempted from listening to our more trivial, foolish and shallow whining. If we must confront God with our criticisms – and of course we must, if we are to be true to the biblical insights that we find in the cries of Job and the Psalmist – then let this confrontation not be at a surface level.

Let it be a deeper cry; one that may conceivably evoke a deeper response.

'Deepening our faith' in these ways will prove to be a challenge. This deeper work is not going to be easy. It will be hard graft, like crafting and jointing legs to a piece of wood to make a table, or forcing ourselves deeper under the waves to explore the mysteries of the seabed, or listening hard to people in the depth of their lives – instead of just chattering on about externals. But most of the worthwhile things in life are that bit harder. And don't we know that appreciating and communicating the depths are among the most worthwhile of human endeavours?

In any case, we have no choice. This is what we are called to work at – the life of this deeper gospel. For if God and truth lie anywhere, they are to be found in the deepnesses of our everyday lives.

3

In and out of the desert

They cannot scare me with their empty spaces
Between stars – on stars where no human race is.
I have it in me so much nearer home
To scare myself with my own desert places.

Robert Frost

The author A. N. Wilson was once abandoned in the Negeb Desert south of Jerusalem for a day and a night. Years later he confessed that the extremes of cold and heat, the clarity of the night sky bright with stars, and his own hunger and thirst gave him 'a small insight into what other writers . . . have said about the desert's capacity to simplify consciousness itself'.

In the Authorized Version of the Bible, the Greek word *erēmia* is translated as 'desert'. It is a word that the New Testament uses to picture an abandoned empty place, one 'without inhabitants' – a wilderness. Our English word similarly stands for an uninhabited, barren, desolate and *deserted* location.

A great deal is said about such places in Scripture. In the Old Testament the desert is the place of Israel's wanderings into sin and grace. Some thought that their Messiah would appear first in the desert. In the New Testament John the Baptist preaches in the desert, and Jesus is driven there 'by the Spirit' to be tested. He is alone in the desert, apart that is from 'the wild beasts' and Satan, the tempter. Afterwards, according to Matthew's Gospel, he is joined there by 'ministering angels'.

27

A remarkable spiritual movement once arose within Christianity, as generations of 'Desert Fathers' followed the third-century St Antony of Egypt in withdrawing to the desert to wrestle against temptation and what they perceived as the deceptions of the Devil, and to learn how to discern authentic religious experience. They chose that destination because, as Rowan Williams writes, 'The desert is a place for overcoming illusions and purifying desire.' The discipline (*akesis*) of the desert is precisely a 'discipline to destroy illusions', by removing the distortions of reality and seeing things as they truly are. It is also, interestingly, a place where we learn not to judge others: for 'true solitude means a refusal to imprison others in your projections'. As another writer (Parker Palmer) puts it, the desert is where 'we must first wrestle with the demons of untruth that arise in the silence, demons that come from our own need to manipulate and master truth rather than let truth transform us'.

Real deserts are extreme, extraordinary places. For most of us they are also geographically distant, and we should have to make a long journey to visit one. Such a desert would seem to be very different from our everyday world.

But the deserts that the poet Robert Frost is thinking of are not so far away. These wildernesses are situations that are *very* familiar, very everyday, very ordinary. They are 'my own desert places'.

Harry Williams' wilderness

When a clergyman of my age and weight begins to talk about such matters, his mind naturally turns to thoughts of another Williams. Harry Williams was a Cambridge don who later became a monk of the Community of the Resurrection at Mirfield in Yorkshire. I met him a couple of times when I was a student, but saw him last on television in a brief cameo performance during the ill-fated marriage of the Prince of Wales and Lady Diana Spencer, when he appeared from a transept of St Paul's Cathedral drowning in a long surplice, to offer some appropriate prayers. It seemed to me then a bizarre image, for Harry Williams was a priest of some notoriety in his day, and hardly an establishment figure. He became well known for his autobiographical honesty and his psychological accounts of Christian doctrine. 'Whatever else theology is', he urged, 'it must in some sense be a theology of the self.' He was admired by many, not least for his insights into the true nature of ministry and his refreshingly debunking attitude to its often bogus authority. He once wrote,

The true priest . . . is anybody who is the channel to others of God's love, and is willing to share something of the cost of that love; and whose eyes are open to perceive God's presence everywhere and in everybody. Priesthood, I believed, and still believe, has nothing to do with entering a special divinely ordained caste.

But it was in another of his many books that he offers material relevant to the theme of this chapter. I refer to a famous sermon, the sort of sermon that many preachers devoutly wished they had written themselves – and some have even pretended that they have – in which Williams preached on the Christian season of Lent in terms of 'the true wilderness'. This is, I think, the authentic voice of an authentic religious experience. It is one aspect of what we might call the *Lenten life*, which is itself a strand of all life.

Lent is supposed to be the time when we think of Jesus in the wilderness. And the wilderness belongs to us. It is always lurking somewhere as part of our experience, and there are times when it seems pretty near the whole of it . . . Most people's wilderness is inside them, not outside . . . Our wilderness . . . is an inner isolation. It's an absence of contact. It's a sense of being alone – boringly alone, or saddeningly alone, or terrifyingly alone.

This is a writer who obviously knows what he is talking about, because he knows it from the inside. He doesn't just know 'about' the wilderness; he has been there. So he is able to describe the interior, internal Lent. 'And so', he writes, 'we are tempted of Satan':

29

Tempted to give up, to despair . . . Tempted to banish from our life all that we hold most dear, and that is love, tempted to lock ourselves up so that when we pass by people feel, 'There goes a dead man.' And behind each and all of these temptations is the temptation to disbelieve in what we are, the temptation to distrust ourselves, to deny that it is the Spirit Himself which beareth witness with our spirit. God in us.

In this sermon Williams rehearses the ancient theme that the wilderness is for us, as it was for Jesus, part of our training – and that training, he promises, 'does not last for ever'. But the Lenten training ground is real enough. It is 'our going with Jesus into the wilderness to be tempted', to be tested, to be proved.

Another great writer on religious experience, Thomas Merton, called this spiritual desert 'the sterile paradise of emptiness and rage'. This inner wilderness is where we are alone, with the wild beasts. And here the central question, as Harry Williams recognized, is this: Is the wilderness a place where the angels will minister to us also? Is God 'in us', even just with us, there?

Alone

Apparently not. The wilderness, rather, is the place where we are alone: 'boringly', 'saddeningly' or 'terrifyingly' alone. Even in the middle of a crowd – at work or play, in a close relationship, in the chaos of a houseful of children – we may find ourselves in such a wilderness. Alone.

Note the kind of language that seems to be most natural to describe this condition: we *find* ourselves alone. 'It is not good that the man be alone,' God reflects at the end of one of the creation stories in the book of Genesis. But, surely, sometimes it is? It is not just celebrities who pout, 'I want to be alone.' We often share that desire, as our non-celebrity world of work clashes around our ears, or the kids press in around our lives, and we yearn for solitude – or bed. 'The world is too much with us; late and soon,' Wordsworth complains. 'Getting and spending, we lay waste our powers.'

So, exhausted and drained, we may in a traditional Christian way seek a 'quiet time' or a retreat; or just get to our bed early.

All of which is fine. These things can certainly help. But I suspect that they can only help if we are really yearning for an *exterior* aloneness. We do often earnestly seek and gratefully embrace that sort of solitude. But I am thinking here of the desert that we do not desire, the wilderness we never seek. This is the one we enter despite ourselves, when we gradually or suddenly just find ourselves alone. It is the inner desert into which we unintentionally slide, rather than the outer one that we may walk towards with eager anticipation.

Although this inner desert is a desert that we have not chosen, it is still our desert: my place, where none else is. This is an experience that is about me and about what it really means, in every sense, to find myself alone.

It is, indeed, a hard and barren place, which we did not seek. Yet it is good for us to be here.

Individuality

Such a claim may raise some hackles. I should emphasize that I am not advocating pure individualism, nor am I arguing for the self-reliance or egoism of the life of an untrammelled free individual who disregards other people. Far from it. The social is the essential context of our everyday, as it is of our evolution as a species and of our nurture as its individual members. Nevertheless, I also ask that we recognize that individuality must have a central place in religion. Elsewhere in this book I shall plead for a personal, particular and distinctive faith, suitable for distinctive, particular and individual persons. I do so in conscious opposition to one of the more irritating of current theological and ecclesiastical fashions, the unremitting emphasis on the cosily communal and general. No doubt 'Christianity is essentially a social religion', as John Wesley (and many others) put it. No doubt we are all called to join a fellowship of disciples; but even that particular cliché implies that the Church actually comes second – second to each individual responding individually to the call of Christ. There must be an essential particularity about the call to discipleship, because there is an essential particularity about people. God calls us by name.

This is one aspect of the truth that is captured in the philosopher A. N. Whitehead's motto that 'religion is what the individual does with his own solitariness'. It is even more central to Kierkegaard's insistence on individual judgement and individual responsibility. He wrote, 'The Christian combat is always waged by the individual; for this precisely is spirit, that everyone is an individual before God, that "fellowship" is a lower category than "the single individual", which everyone can be and should be.' For Kierkegaard, 'Eternity' asks what we did, what we were, and not about how we were related to the ideas of others, to popular opinion, to 'the frivolous crowd'. 'The all-knowing One . . . does not desire the crowd. He desires the individual; He will deal only with the individual.' In eternity, Kierkegaard insists, crowds do not exist, for 'Eternity scatters the crowd by giving each infinite weight . . . as an individual.'

C. S. Lewis puts a similar theme into the mouth of Aslan, in his Narnia chronicle, *The Horse and His Boy*:

'And I was the lion you do not remember who pushed the boat in which you lay, a child near death, so that it came to shore where a man sat, wakeful at midnight, to receive you.'

'Then it was you who wounded Aravis?'

'It was I.'

'But what for?'

'Child,' said the Voice, 'I am telling you your story, not hers. I tell no one any story but his own.'

The first rule of the spiritual life is not to look over your shoulder to see what the others are doing, and certainly not to see what they are getting (thus Matthew 20.1–16). It is as if God says, 'This is about you and me. What I pay the other labourers in the vineyard is not your concern.' Hence the second rule of the spiritual life is that we should not be tempted to think that the grass over the fence is any greener than the stuff we are munching on ourselves. This is a good rule, since it very rarely actually is any better, even though for the moment it may look that way. (How many times do we find ourselves overtaken by guilt, having assumed for so long that someone's life was easier or more blessed than our own, and then finding out what that life is really like – or what it has suddenly become?)

In the days when the local vicar still regularly risked the 'cold calling' of house-to-house visiting in his parish, many a conversation on the doorstep would end before it had begun with the parishioner demurring at talking about religion, on the grounds that 'it's too personal'. That reaction is much more common today. I believe that this refusal is not simply a function of our culture's radical privatization of religion or our innate British reticence. It is also, at least in some small part, an authentically religious reaction. At any rate, I have more sympathy with it than many have. It seems to me that there is a proper distaste that prevents our allowing any public exploration of the inner anatomy of our souls. This is akin to the reluctance we sometimes feel to listen in on the messier details of the sins and inadequacies of other people. Such matters, we think – when we are at our best – should properly be left to God. And we are right. Who else can truly understand another? Who else knows how special we are?

True religion sees and celebrates the individuality and the uniqueness of all human kind. In doing this it lauds the variety of form in creation, and the exotic diversity of God's activity. It is multidimensional. False religion, by contrast, knows only one dimension. It insists that there is to be only one kind of human being, or at least only one kind of Christian. Like Procrustes, the mythological Stretcher, it will only tolerate guests who fit its bed exactly. This robber of Greek legend seems to have adopted the maxim that, although they had *not* made their own beds, his guests must yet lie tidily upon them. He encouraged this state of affairs by stretching their bodies or chopping bits off until they fitted his furniture more snugly.

Too much of religion is Procrustean. I'm fed up with it; it is a travesty. A Procrustean religion produces a semblance of uniformity only by doing violence to people. It results, if I may shift the metaphor from mythology to genetics, in a cloned Church. And clones, of course, being genetically identical, can never adapt to new circumstances. They can never evolve; and species that do not evolve eventually die out as the world around them changes. The success of any cloned Church will therefore be short-lived.

Churches need to contain a wider variety of religious individuals than they often allow.

Religion is intensely individual partly because it is of the heart and personal, and thus 'of or for a particular person'. Mine is therefore different from yours, however loudly we confess the same creed and however punctiliously we enact the same rituals. Admittedly, God calls individuals to move on and change; but that is a call to 'become themselves', to become as God intends them to be. God calls them first where they are, as they are. He asks each one, 'Who do you think you are?', and expects an answer. While everybody knows this, we do not always remember that God will accept our answer, whatever it is. And that God always then responds with a second invitation: '*You* come, then. Follow me.'

Which brings us back to the desert; for the desert faith is also about individuals, although it is an individualistic theme of a more harrowing kind.

The desert we must contemplate here is one where each of us is alone, and therefore necessarily an individual; but one in which we can take no comfort at all. This is not the chosen solitude and restful peace of the moorland walk, the silent retreat or even the bed of exhaustion. This is the aloneness that recalls our birth and anticipates our death. These two events 'happen to us', and happen to each of us in our ultimate aloneness – however many may cluster around the bed. As the nineteenth-century poet Matthew Arnold complained:

34

YES! in the sea of life enisled,
With echoing straits between us thrown,
Dotting the shoreless watery wild,
We mortal millions live *alone* . . .

Who ordered, that their longing's fire
Should be, as soon as kindled, cooled?
Who renders vain their deep desire? –
A God, a God their severance ruled!
And bade betwixt their shores to be
The unplumbed, salt, estranging sea.

Words like these may push us towards despair as we come to acknowledge our ultimate aloneness. But such realism need not be wholly negative. Indeed, if it is truly realistic, it cannot be. At any rate, those who have been into the desert and come back out again often speak of something more positive and creative, even hopeful. For this solitude can be, in Henri Nouwen's words, 'the furnace of transformation . . . the place of the great struggle and the great encounter'.

In the desert we may hope for some sort of flourishing and some measure of gain.

The sound of silence

Another nineteenth-century English poet, Thomas Hood, wrote of the desert as a place inevitably marked by silence.

There is a silence where hath been no sound,
There is a silence where no sound may be,
In the cold grave – under the deep, deep sea,
Or in wide desert where no life is found . . .

The idea of silence might seem entirely negative. Yet Ammonas, a disciple of Antony, held the view that 'it was by silence that the saints grew'. Out of the silence came something very positive – growth, spiritual growth. But how can this be? And how can it work for us?

Simply stated, it is because in the desert there is no one else. We may talk there, because we can and because we have to. But we talk alone. In Willy Russell's play and film, Shirley Valentine talked to her wall in her desert – because she had to. Hers too was a talking-into-the-silence. And that, surely, is at the heart of all prayer.

Prayer is where we become ourselves. In prayer you form and reform a self that is not less than all the other selves you are when other people are around, but is a self that is both these and yet more than these – beyond these. Harry Williams says this of prayer: 'Prayer is the means by which we become aware of the final me. Prayer is going down deep into myself to the place where I can find the final me. Prayer is anything which puts me in touch with the final me.' This final, ultimate, decisive, real me is the self that can speak of itself only to itself, in the silence and alone. To do that is to speak to *God*; for in the context of prayer, according to the Catholic theologian Gareth Moore, God is 'the one we are with when we are with *nobody*'.

So, in the desert we pray. There is nothing else that we can do.

Now prayer is not a highly specialized, esoteric skill. Rather, it is very ordinary, natural, everyday stuff. It is just talking. Sometimes it is just thinking. Sometimes, even, it is just being ourselves. 'In the desert,' writes Ken Leech, 'one is *confronted* by oneself.' There are no secrets in the desert because there cannot be. In my desert, there is just me and God. And it makes no sense psychologically to try to hide anything from ourselves, as it makes no sense theologically to try to hide anything from God.

We speak, then, into the silence. And the silence hears and receives it all, and the silence says (of course) . . . nothing.

This is the most painful part. Nevertheless, I believe that it is also the most significant feature of prayer and of the desert, out there (or, rather, in here) in 'a silence where no sound may be'. It is vitally important for us truthfully to acknowledge this *nothing*.

Do not think that I am unaware of the idea of God answering prayer. I do know about those flushes of emotion that lead to hearts being strangely moved, which provoke conversions and the felt certainty of acceptance. I know about the gracious bestowal of charismatic gifts, divine words and revelations. I know about these things because I have experienced them, as maybe you have. But I also know that they can prove to be misleading, and sometimes in the end illusory; as maybe you do too.

Remember, the desert is 'a place for overcoming illusions'.

So I would argue that, as we speak into the silence when we are at our most alone, we must learn *to hear the silence*. We must not rush to fill it ourselves; for that would be to take it too lightly, not to take it seriously. Nor should we strain our ears to hear something other than the silence, because that can so easily be the doorway into fantasy. And fantasy is something that we very much need to avoid, for there is quite enough of it about in religion already. As another has put it, 'What counts is not the magnitude of one's credulity, but the stringency and integrity of faith' – hence, 'there must be no more pixie-dust.'

In the desert you will hear only your own voice, your own honest voice. And then, the silence.

But you must also hear the silence as a reply.

Spiritual hearing

Prayer is largely a matter simply of being ourselves. In our desert, it involves praying the prayer of the one who is alone, speaking the truth before God. However weary, even bitter that prayer may be, it is still a prayer. It is still a yearning.

The poets know best how to express this. In the prayer of the twentieth-century poet Gavin Ewart, the use of the verb 'to desert' reminds us that this is the root of the noun 'desert' (the forsaken place). Ewart requests, in puzzlement and perhaps fear, that God should not desert his wilderness.

O Lord you have it in your power to hurt me
O Lord in your odd way please do not desert me.

But it is that extraordinary Welsh poet and Anglican priest, R. S. Thomas, who captures most powerfully our pain of praying into the silence.

> What listener
> is this, who is always awake
> and says nothing? His breathing
> is the rising and falling of oceans on remote
> stars . . .
> I lift my face
> to a face, its features dissolving
> in the radiation out of a black hole.

In his earlier poems, while Thomas famously wrote of God as 'that great absence / In our lives, the empty silence / Within', he also acknowledged that:

> It is this great absence
> that is like a presence, that compels
> me to address it without hope
> of a reply . . .

So, then, in the desert we pray.

And whatever else we pray, we pray something like this. For all prayer, in the end, is this – and nothing more: 'Here I am. I am like this. I know it. You know it. What now?'

We pray 'without hope of a reply'. And yet, don't we hear something? Religious hearing, I would say, is partly a question of correctly hearing the silence of the desert.

So what does this silence say to our prayer? Perhaps this:

> And *I* am like this. Beyond anything you can conceive. Utterly different from your imaginings; best described in silence.
> You know it. Well, accept it.
> Accept the mystery and accept my gifts to you. Accept your life.
> And accept my silence.

Accepting in the end

The end of prayer, like the end of life, is a matter of acceptance. Not at first, of course. At first – and often for a long time – we may need to struggle. We must first rebel and strive to change things, since this world is not perfect, it is not even just – and we must toil to make it, wherever and whenever possible, nearer to that ideal. We must work hard to force things a little closer to God's heart's desire, and to strive to understand his mystery.

But, in the end, all toil must cease. And then, what can there be, except acceptance? God says:

> At the end, this is what it is like. I know it. You know it. So accept it. Accept especially the silence.
>
> You ask, 'What now?' *Anything*. Any thing can happen. You already know that; but perhaps you do not yet know that you will be able to bear anything that happens, if only you can come to accept even this silence as being from the hand of your God.

Carlo Carretto is one of the Little Brothers of Jesus of Charles de Foucauld who combine work with the poor and deprived with a contemplative life and lengthy retreats in the desert (this time a real desert – the Sahara). He writes here of being wrapped in 'God's impenetrable night', and of its 'terrible loneliness' and sense of abandonment.

> In this deeply painful state, prayer becomes true and strong even though it may be as dry as dust.
>
> The soul speaks to its God out of its poverty and pain; still more out of its impotence and abjection . . .
>
> Deep down the soul has understood that it must let itself be carried, that it must abandon itself to its Saviour, that alone it can do nothing, that God can do everything.

'What matters', he writes, 'is to let God get on with it.' This is true religious acceptance. It is an acceptance of the silence in which God gets on with what *God* gets on with.

And that, possibly, is the moment when the wild beasts turn into the ministering angels; it is the moment when we accept the given-ness of our life, as from the hand of God. And then, as Leech puts it, the spiritual desert becomes 'the place of *katharsis*, of stripping and nakedness, of man's terrible aloneness and God's mysterious reveal-ing.' This is the sort of moment that fits Harry Williams' arresting words: the moment when 'Lent, we discover, is Easter in disguise.'

On moving in and out

Finally, however, what about this language of going 'in' and coming 'out', from the title of this chapter?

As I have already indicated, I think of 'going into' the desert in terms of making a virtue out of a necessity. We find ourselves there on the unstable scree, sliding out into the wilderness. (A friend, spotting 'In and Out of the Desert' advertised as my theme for the talk on which this chapter is based, quipped that it looked like a slippery topic, this movement 'in and out of the dessert'. Of course, she was right – even with the correct spelling.)

I am a great moaner, as you may be too. I find it hard to accept the inevitable; and very hard to accept the unacceptable. But even I must allow that in the end there is no alternative. So we must accept the slipping too.

The spiritual life is finally about acceptance. The grass will always seems greener somewhere else, whether that somewhere else is Egypt or the Promised Land. At least both locations have grass, unlike this desolate, deserted place. But Israel was called to wander 40 years in the desert between enslavement and settlement, so as to find – and to be found by – God. They found him in the desert, as and when they at last found themselves. Both findings were unexpected dis-coveries. Stuck in the desert, they slipped into faith. Is that how we should think of revelation?

But what about the 'going out'? Spiritually speaking, deserts are not for living in but for learning in. We are called to live in society and to love in society. And therefore we are called back out of our desert.

In our own lives it may be that we will repeatedly, even monotonously, go in and come out of our inner desert; or perhaps the desert will be for us just an occasional, special excursion. In either case, after we have come out, we must remember that we were in there once. I know someone who once publicly shared his spiritual distress and loss of faith. I met him again a couple of years later, and privately asked how things were now. He remembered nothing, or at least he acknowledged nothing, of his desert wanderings. Indeed, later that day I heard him speak vehemently against those who 'challenged faith'. I found it all very sad.

There is already too much pretence in too much of religion. Let us not pretend to one another like that. Especially let us not pretend that there are no deserts. For the desert is inside all of us. And *sometimes* it will bloom like no other part of our world.

In the seventeenth century, the celebrated poet and priest John Donne captured the truth of this, as he often did:

> Churches are best for prayer, that have least light:
> To see God only, I go out of sight:
> And to 'scape stormy days, I choose
>   An everlasting night.

4

With friends like these . . .

The only way to have a friend is to be one.
Ralph Waldo Emerson

The complete version of the traditional saying from which I have extracted my chapter title is, of course, 'With friends like these, who needs enemies?' It is very widely employed (an Internet search revealed over 36,000 web pages that quote it), but in a Christian context it is hard not to see its natural application as being to Jesus' disciples. It also, therefore, refers to us.

Aristotle regarded friendship as a supremely important virtue; he wrote that a friend is to each person 'another self', one who enables us to know our own lives properly. Life could not be complete, he argued, without friendship. John Dryden adds to the concept a religious connotation, describing friendship as 'a holy tie'.

Friendship is central to the lives of most people. Because of this unavoidable truth, it is also central to our everyday spirituality, and to learning Christ in the ordinary way.

Biblical friends?

On this assumption, I thought that I ought to do a little research on the topic within the Christian tradition. I began by looking at five Bible dictionaries. There was nothing relevant in any of them. Trawling more widely, I did manage to run the concept to ground in *The Oxford Dictionary of the Christian Church*. Or, rather, I found in that classic reference text three entries on societies which had the word 'friend' in their title: the 'Society of Friends' (the Quakers), the 'Friends of God' (the *Gottesfreunde* – a fourteenth-century lay devotional movement in Continental Europe) and that other most holy and spiritual of organizations, the 'Friends of the Cathedrals'.

At this stage in my studies I was tempted to fall back on a cynical form of the argument from silence; for if the scholars of religion did not think friendship important enough to mention, then it must be really important. Pressing on, however, I eventually picked up references to friendship in SCM's *Dictionary of Christian Spirituality*, and another in the 1913 edition of Hastings' *Dictionary of Religion and Ethics*. It was in this last, aged source that I was finally rewarded by a quotation worth quoting (originally from the *Jewish Encyclopedia*): 'The Bible endows friendship with a peculiar dignity by making it symbolical of the intimacy that exists between God and man.'

Despite its dated language, I felt that here at last was someone who agreed on the religious import of this theme and traced it back to the Bible. So, having got my eye in, and forgetting that one should quit while ahead, I buckled down to tackle the great 'Kittel' – the ten-volume reference source of New Testament Greek words and concepts. But there I was to be disappointed again, and this time not by silence but more harshly, by an explicit denial; for the entry by Gustav Stählin describes friendship as 'fundamentally alien' to the Old Testament world. Modern scholarship, it would appear, concedes no scriptural authority for a 'peculiar dignity' for friendship.

Can this be right? After all, it is the Old Testament that calls Abraham, and even his offspring, God's friend (Isaiah 41.8 and 2 Chronicles 20.7); and it is in its pages that God is said to speak to Moses 'as one speaks to his friend' (Exodus 33.11). It is there that the Psalmist bewails the fact that his 'bosom friend in whom I trusted' has turned against him (Psalm 41.9) and Job complains that even his friends scorn him (Job 16.2). Elsewhere in the Hebrew Scriptures prudent advice is on offer both about our choice of friends and about the nature of friendship. For example, Proverbs 18.24 counsels, 'Some friends play at friendship but a true friend sticks closer than one's nearest kin'; and Proverbs 27.6 insists that 'well meant are the wounds a friend inflicts'.

Even those who know little beyond a Sunday-school introduction to the Bible are probably aware of the legendary friendship between David and Jonathan, the son of King Saul. Jonathan is said to have loved David 'as his own soul' (1 Samuel 18.1), and after his friend's death David laments, 'your love to me was wonderful, passing the love of women' (2 Samuel 1.26). Most will also be familiar with the classic account of female friendship in the book of Ruth, where that widow's love for her mother-in-law Naomi leads her to exclaim, 'Where you go I will go . . . your people shall be my people, and your God my God' (Ruth 1.16).

What about the New Testament? It is true that love is the more significant category there, and love goes beyond friendship (cf. Luke 14.12) – since the love that is captured by the Greek word *agapé* is inclusive, whereas friendship is inevitably exclusive. But the theme of friendship flourishes in these books also. Significantly, Jesus is berated for being a friend, or at least for befriending the politically, morally and religiously disloyal tax collectors and other 'sinners' (Matthew 11.19). Jesus thinks it natural to seek help from friends: 'Suppose one of you has a friend, and you go to him at midnight' (Luke 11.5). Although the friend who is thus wakened gets up and opens the bread bin in response to the other's importunity, rather than from the motive power of friendship (v. 8), the friendship is still assumed. Friendship is stretched in such circumstances and its limits are recognized, but it does not break. What lies in the background here, even Stählin admits, is 'the idea that God is the best friend who grants the request of his friend and who indeed wants to be asked'. The character of God is thus partly rendered by the image of friendship.

Disciple–friends

However, the key texts on friendship in the New Testament relate to the disciples. Luke has Jesus calling them 'friends' (Luke 12.4), a word that is applied in John's Gospel to 'our friend Lazarus' (John 11.11). In the book of Acts (27.3) the community of disciples are still being described as 'friends' to one another, and in the Johannine letters we come across such concluding salutations as 'the friends send their greetings' and 'greet the friends' (3 John v. 15). Admittedly, the term may be used quite neutrally as a general salutation – as at Matthew 22.12 and Luke 14.10, and even Matthew 26.50 (where Jesus uses it to Judas in Gethsemane) – but often much more is meant than this. And in John's Gospel we find the true extent of that 'more':

> No one has greater love than this, to lay down one's life for one's friends. You are my friends if you do what I command you. I do not call you servants any longer, because the servant does not know what the master is doing; but I have called you friends, because I have made known to you everything that I have heard from my Father. You did not choose me but I chose you. And I appointed you to go and bear fruit, fruit that will last . . . I am giving you these commands so that you may love one another.
> (John 15.13–17)

Although this is not a 'friendship of equals', it *is* a friendship. It is certainly much more than a master–servant relationship.

Yet if Jesus calls his disciples friends, he must know the risks; he must know that he is bestowing the title on people who will fail at it. According to the Synoptic tradition (in the three 'Synoptic Gospels' of Matthew, Mark and Luke), his friends repeatedly misunderstand him. They jostle for position; one of them eats with Jesus only as a preliminary to betraying him; another (ironically, he is designated 'The Rock') is firm on only one point in his time of testing – 'I do not know this man you are talking about' (Mark 14.71).

With friends like these, who indeed needs enemies?

For all that, let us remember that they are the first saints. The honesty in these accounts of biblical friends is therefore rather striking. Usually saints are written up in plaster, as too good to be true, so that it's tempting to extend the well-known series 'lies, damn lies and statistics' and incorporate, at the next level of deceitfulness, 'hagiography'. This idealization, even falsification, of the saints starts in the New Testament itself. The author of Mark's Gospel is not embarrassed to record some blunt words from disciples terrified by a storm at sea, 'Teacher, do you not care that we are perishing?' Luke, however, tones this down to read, 'Master, Master, we are perishing!'; and the version of the same story in Matthew's Gospel has the disciples piously mouthing, 'Lord, save us! We are perishing!' (Mark 4.38; Luke 8.24; Matthew 8.25).

On the whole, however, the biblical saints are portrayed with brutal frankness; and these candid, unimpressive portraits from the New Testament, which paint them with warts and worse, compare favourably in their honesty with later bowdlerized accounts. We should welcome their stark focus. It is a tradition that is rather touchingly reflected in the portrait of Jesus' disciples in the rock musical *Jesus Christ Superstar*, singing drunkenly after the Last Supper. They'd always hoped they would be apostles so that they could write the Gospels when they retire, and 'they'll still talk about us when we've died.' While Tim Rice's words present an anachronistic and unkind view, it is not a wholly unfair one. For the disciples are sinful saints, remedial learners. In short, they are *failed friends*.

Faithful friends?

And that *is* a comfort, actually. Because despite their failings, it is to his friends that Jesus returns. Jesus, at any rate, is a faithful friend.

If we are lucky, we will know somebody of the type ourselves. I am thinking of the friend who rings first or who forgives first; and the one who listens longest to our rantings, and is still there when the others have made their excuses and left. The friend you can rely on. Rely on for what? Rely on to remain a friend, I suppose; but that is no small thing, for friendship is a high and holy calling, and (regrettably) some people do not seem to understand it.

And what about me? Being male is a poor excuse, but on the whole men do not do friendship well. The newspaper columnist Laura Marcus sarcastically writes that 'their idea of a best friend is someone they haven't seen for ten years'. That's just a bit too close for comfort. As my only 'contact' with one particular friend for the last 30-odd years has been through a Christmas card sent by his divorced wife, I too have my doubts about male friendship. Nor can I cast the first stone myself, not after discovering some years ago that my designated 'Best Friend', in the sense of my most frequently used phone number according to British Telecommunications' 'Friends & Family' discount system, turned out to be my current dial-up Internet service provider. That sort of thing makes you think.

I was once taught by a lecturer who was not only a great name-dropper, but also claimed to know personally everyone that anybody mentioned. Students who went to conferences to hear some internationally renowned theologian would be told that Professor X, Y or Z was 'a great friend of mine – so be sure to remember me to him'. The more innocent acted on this suggestion, only to be met by blank stares and the response, in various degrees of broken English, 'I am sorry, *who* . . . ?'

In part these difficulties derive from the fact that the word 'friend' is vague in its application, like the word 'bald'. Some people seem willing to apply such terms so widely that they lose their descriptive point. To get anywhere in this discussion of friendship we shall need to concentrate on what most people would think of as *close* friends, *real* friends. As Aristotle insisted, real friendship is only possible with a few. Here quality, rather than quantity, is the rule.

What is it that marks out such an intimate relationship? According to the quotable nineteenth-century American essayist Emerson, it is the twin properties of 'truth' and 'tenderness'. Truth does seem to be part of the equation. For C. S. Lewis, the real question in friendship is, 'Do you see the same truth?' If we see wholly different truths, we shall never be friends. Yet there is a danger in this claim. It cannot mean that we will always agree with a friend, because we won't. Perhaps honesty is a more significant word here. (Emerson himself glosses the word 'truth' with 'sincerity': 'A friend is a person with whom I may be sincere.') Friends can, and sometimes must, disagree; but they can and must be honest enough to allow such disagreements, if they are to remain friends. They must be honest enough to say, 'No, I *don't* see it that way.'

What about tenderness? Friendship, Emerson says, 'is for aid and comfort'; it therefore serves not only 'for serene days' but also for 'rough roads and hard fare'. For the Canadian philosopher Donald Evans, friendliness is one of those deep dispositions that undergird both religion and morality, which he calls 'attitude-virtues'. He ranks alongside it trust, humility and responsibility, and a range of other stances for living. Like Emerson, Evans claims that friendliness is a species of love (along with concern and contemplation), and therefore treats it as one of the goals of human life. It involves a giving and receiving 'at a very deep personal level'. My friend confirms me, Evans writes; she or he 'is *with* me, *for* me'. But because this is so, a friend is someone who may challenge me without condemnation. Sometimes I can only really hear – and bear – the criticism of a person who loves me. This is real affection; it is something strong, rather than anything soppy.

Variety and life

Part of the power and significance of friends appears to be that they are chosen. That, of course, makes them very different from relatives. BT's 'Friends & Family' category is actually rather an unstable mixed economy. The company once made a surprising offer, advertising that your 'Friends & Family' group were eligible to win a joint holiday away. Some prize! In most cases it is difficult enough when the whole family ventures out together; disaster would be the only sure result of adding your friends to the excursion.

It is a fairly safe prediction that few of your relatives would get on with any of your friends, partly because your friends rarely have much in common with your family. Actually, friends often have little in common with one another, despite those claims about their 'seeing the same truth'. A house party composed of all your friends might be successful, but only if your friends are all pipe-smoking, tweedy, donnish Tolkien-esque middle-class Englishmen (or whatever). Using the same logic, a girls'-night-out might work if you and your girl friends all like to do the same things on a night out. But many groups of friends are just too diverse for this all-embracing, communal chumminess.

My friends, at least, have little in common with one another; and yet I have chosen each one of them. On what grounds? I hardly know how to answer. I like him for his likeableness. I value her for her valuable characteristics. Those two are admired for their admirability. I only know that they are all different, as different as the different qualities I appreciate in people. For the author of Ecclesiasticus (one of the apocryphal books of the Old Testament), 'faithful friends are life-saving medicine' (Sirach 6.16) – which suggests that each is something of a tonic, at the very least. And we know that medicines need to be as varied as the illnesses they treat, and indeed as life itself. Here is a theme to which we shall return.

If we find ourselves with different friends it is partly because we like different things, and because each of us likes a variety of different things – and likes them at different times. As Michel de Montaigne, the great sixteenth-century French essayist, noted, with regard to his closest friend, 'If I were pressed to say why I love him, I feel that my only reply could be: "Because it was he, because it was I." ' So, although I may remain the same, the differences in the nature of the 'hes' and 'shes' will account for the variety of my friends.

It is possible that this variety may recall us to something deeper, as Evans suggests. True friendship is more than a rewarding relationship, it is a commitment to a person. And that means that we accept them for what they are. Each of them, as they are. We respect their privacy and their freedom, their getting-on-with-their-lives without us. In a word – Evans' word – we celebrate the very existence of our friends; we are glad that they are alive, and not just for our benefit. 'Friendliness . . . involves a *celebration* of the strengths of another person for their own sake.'

Interest in friendship

It would be naïve to deny that we are friends with a person partly because we 'get something out of' the relationship. At the most basic level, we enjoy their company. But this interested affection, in which we have and find an 'interest' (something for us), is heavily qualified in true friendship. True friendship has a *disinterested* element too, transcending any ulterior purpose. This is not at all a matter of being '*un*interested' in our friend, but – as the dictionary puts it – of being 'not influenced by one's own advantage' with regard to the friendship. Real friendship involves a hefty dose of disinterested celebration of the uniqueness of the other, and of the variety of the others. In friendship we go beyond liking other people. We rejoice in them.

The philosopher H. H. Price argued that the way in which we 'believe in' our friends (the way we are in favour of them, 'for' them and trust them) is our best analogy for our belief in God.

As soon as we start thanking God for his gifts, being grateful for them with a gratitude which is not just 'a lively sense of favours to come', our belief in God ceases to be wholly interested. We are beginning to value God for God's own sake, and to believe that it is a good thing, intrinsically good, that God exists and God is what he is; and not just 'a good thing', but the fundamental 'good thing' without which there would be no others.

At this stage, the nearest analogue in inter-human relationships would be belief in a friend, where there is a similar combination of interested and disinterested believing-in. It is perhaps significant that some theistic mystics have referred to God as 'The Friend'.

The God whom we (quite naturally) love on account of his goodness towards us, we must learn to love for himself. Thomas Aquinas noted the parallel with friendship, and developed it quite sensitively. Friends 'really converse' together, he wrote; they 'delight' in each other's presence, they 'rejoice' in each other's actions and their talk. We find security in the friend 'against all anxieties'; friends also 'agree together'. It is in this way, says Thomas, that 'the Holy Spirit constitutes us God's friends'.

These elements of friendliness are to be found on both sides of divine–human friendship. How do I relate to my friends? I confirm them, sometimes I gently confront them, and I celebrate them. I am loyal to them; I seek to be close to them; I refuse to manipulate them. (Well, I know that is how I should behave.) And with God? Evans writes:

> In so far as I am friendly towards God I confirm his existence, acknowledging that he is distinct from me – indeed he is the very 'ground' on which I stand. I confront God, calling him to task for many of the injustices and tragedies of human life . . . I celebrate God's existence in worship, devote myself to him in loyalty and attention, respectfully refrain from trying to manipulate his power, and affectionately seek closeness with him by being close to his creatures.

But in what way is God 'friends' with us? According to Evans, the disciple trusts that God 'confirms, confronts, and celebrates his human friends, treating each with devotion, respect and affection'. If this is so, then the relationship is like a truly *adult* friendship. And it is this adult understanding of mutual friendship that makes it preferable to the more one-sided parent–child relationship as a model for our relationship with God.

The twelfth-century Aelred, Abbot of Rievaulx, celebrated human friendship both as a reflection of the love of God, and as having its source and end in God. For Aelred, friendship is a place where we may learn Christ. Christ himself kisses us, he appears to argue, in the love of our friends. 'Here we are, you and I, and I hope Christ makes a third with us.' 'Those whom friendship joins together, it immerses in the contemplation of God.' Indeed, 'God is friendship.' Centuries later, the poet and Catholic martyr Robert Southwell wrote in a poem in praise of Christ: 'First Friend He was, best Friend He is, all times will try Him true.'

On having favourites

But just a minute. Does this talk of divine friendship not smack of a certain favouritism on God's part? And isn't that rather suspect? (Presumably favouritism isn't anything we should be wary of on *our* part; no one would criticize a person for having God as her 'favourite friend'.)

I need now to revisit a point that I rather glossed over earlier. I once saw a TV documentary in which an Aga-and-Volvo-enhanced middle-class couple were discussing their children. 'We love Tabitha best', the female partner prated (fortunately I have forgotten the real names of their children), 'because she is very clever with her hands; and we love Michael best, because he is so kind to animals; and we love Russell best, because...' It was all deeply irritating. Nevertheless, it captured a profound truth: that we do not rank our children all on the same scale. Each may be seen, each one must be seen, as having his or her own 'way of being best'. Our children cannot be measured together; they are, to use the jargon, 'incommensurable'. To some degree this is because our children have different virtues and these virtues are incommensurable – as are their vices also. They cannot all be measured against the same standard.

And so it is with our friends, which is why I found myself using similar language on p. 49 above. Do we, in fact, really have 'best friends'; or is that only a possibility for young children or those seeking to comply with the artificial categories of BT's database? Isn't a best friend as strange a notion as a 'best' or 'favourite' drink? (Where and when? Before, during or after dinner? On a frosty January evening in Scotland, or at a Mediterranean poolside bar at high noon in summer?) Go on, then, answer the daft magazine quiz if you must. Tell them what your favourite piece of music is, or your favourite item of clothing, or your favourite book (or even your 'favourite word', for goodness' sake, as in one I spotted recently). 'It all depends', surely; although few questionnaires allow us to say so. It all depends on when and where and how we feel. And it is the same with what and whom we want to be with, or talk to, or even play out with, at any given time.

These comments run the danger of being understood as postmodern sloppiness, eclectic grazing at the pick-and-mix counter set up to tempt the palates of those who lack any settled standards of taste. But that would be to adopt the relativistic mindset of the slightly jaded, not-really-bothered undecided. 'Well, I don't know what to have,' they mutter. 'Maybe a few aniseed balls, a couple of mint imperials and half a scoop of chocolate brazils?' In such a case it doesn't matter what we choose. But 'it all depends' can be a much more serious response than that (see Chapter 7).

It may be true that we choose our friends, yet we don't choose among or between our friends – not deeply, not decisively, not evaluatively. Our friends are not to be measured together. And that means that they are not to be set one over against another – which is why one friend should never be seen as any sort of threat by another.

So, possibly, we should not ask so wooden a question as, 'Has God any favourites, any "best friends"?'

It may be true, however, that some people do not seem to be befriended by God at all. In the eighteenth century, the rationalistic critics of religion took fierce moral offence at the doctrine of particular revelation and the claim that God acted in history on behalf of particular people. Such theologies portrayed a partiality of the worst kind. ('How odd of God to choose the Jews.') 'It cannot be that [God] would bestow a favour upon any, unless he bestowed the same upon all,' is how the Anglican divine Joseph Butler reported their criticisms. His own work – written in his rectory in the village of Stanhope in the Durham dales – rejected that view as incompatible with how God works in the natural world. As Butler pointed out, God creates some beautiful and others ugly, some weak and sickly and others strong and healthy. Unfairness seems to be built in to things. (Clearly this raises further problems, which we must face in the next chapter.)

Traditional theology has made much of the freedom of God's choice or 'election'. The implication of this doctrine is that, although it may be a matter of regret if you are left out of God's circle, there is no excuse for crowing if you find that you have been included. Exclusion or inclusion are not factors over which you can exercise any real control or claim any brownie points, for God's choice is never a response to our worthiness, but a free, gratuitous gift. Anyway, boasting that 'she counts me a friend', rather than just rejoicing in it, is an attitude that is alien to and destructive of human friendship; so it is likely that it will also erode our relationship with God. In both cases, to employ Montaigne's language, friendship ultimately springs into life 'because it was He', rather than 'because it was I'. The parallel here is so close to the divine case that some have claimed, with Emerson, 'My friends have come to me unsought. The great God gave them to me.'

Even so, friendship brings responsibilities, as does any form of love. That, at least, is what Israel was told when God chose this unworthy nation to be his beacon, servant and priest to the world. And it is what Israel, according to its prophets, tried very hard to forget. It is also what Jesus' disciples signally failed to realize, until much later – when many of them did eventually drink the cup that he had drunk and were baptized with his baptism (cf. Mark 10.38).

We should beware of lightly embracing friendship. The introduction to the Marriage Service in the 1662 Book of Common Prayer rightly warns us that we shouldn't seek to grasp even at true love, 'unadvisedly, lightly, or wantonly'. If we act like that in any real relationship, it is possible that we shall crush it – or vice versa. The prayer-complaint of the sixteenth-century Spanish nun, St Teresa of Avila, illustrates that even friendship with God is a mixed blessing. She is said to have voiced it while falling from her donkey cart into the mud. 'If this is how you treat your friends, no wonder you have so few.' But then, aren't all our blessings mixed?

There is a sense, however, in which whether I become a friend of God does depend partly on me. This is where the element of 'because it was I' comes into play. Friendship, after all, is gift and response. It is not rape; God forces no one. One could say that, although God offers friendship to all, only some take up the offer. Thus, while God's friendship-circle is in practice limited and particular, it is also in principle universal and limitless. Presumably, that was Jesus' way. He offered an unconditional embrace, creating what the theologian Jürgen Moltmann calls 'open friendship'. This is a relationship that respects the other person so much that she has the space to be herself, to be 'other' and to keep her identity – and therefore the space to resist God's embrace. And that is how our friendships should be.

What about 'choice', then? There are some friends whom we can be said to choose in the strong sense that we seek them out and initiate the relationship – metaphorically stretching out our hand towards them. But other friends may more properly be said to choose us, as they respond to our more general, wide-ranging, more or less indiscriminate, 'friendliness'. With these other friends *our* decisive choice is expressed in grasping the hand that they extend to us. But, in both cases, there is some element of choice on our friend's side. No one is in the end compelled; all must choose us too.

Maybe we should not think that God has favourites, but that there are some who warm to the smile of his grace more than others, responding more readily to his ever outstretched hand by offering their own.

Be there for me

Two final points. The American poet Walt Whitman wrote of his own friends: 'I have perceived that to be with those I like is enough . . . I do not ask any more delight, I swim in it as in a sea.' It just feels good to be with friends, especially when nothing more is expected on either side. It is a joy to share a meal or a drink with them, or even a holiday. These things – whatever people say – are *free*, not because someone does not have to pay, but because they form no part of a system of exchange or expectation. Emerson again: 'The essence of friendship is entireness, a total magnanimity and trust.' As Bors de Ganys, a cousin of Lancelot, puts it in Richard Hovey's play: 'Friendship is as God, who gives and asks no payment.' Gifts between friends are real gifts, for nothing is expected in return. 'You don't have to *do* anything; just be there for me and with me,' our friends say. (Or, more probably, they don't; not in our culture, and especially if they are male – although younger people now speak a lot more explicitly about their relationships. Anyway, that is what they all mean.) 'Just *be* there . . .'

It is so with God, also. At the end of all of Job's protesting, he gets a good telling-off out of the whirlwind (Job 38—41). Who knows why? Job doesn't; or at least he shouldn't, for God has not actually answered any of Job's very reasonable complaints about the injustice of his suffering. Yet somehow it doesn't matter. Sometimes, it seems, even a telling-off is enough. It is sufficient that God cares enough to come by, to avow his presence. To this extent, at least, the mysterious, all-powerful Creator has behaved like a proper friend. He has come to be with us in our pain. As George MacDonald puts it: ' "O God!" I cried and that was all. But what are the prayers of the whole universe more than expansion of that one cry? It is not what God can give us, but God that we want.'

The other point is this: friends treasure what we care about. What the world thinks counts, of course it does. But it deep-down matters what our friends think of us. This is a matter of *real mattering*; and real mattering is what matters most. The British Prime Minister, A. S. Balfour, encouraged his contemporaries with the aphorism that 'nothing matters very much and very few things matter at all'. But boy, one is tempted to respond, those things that do, *do*. What our friends think is important to us. This is an intrinsic part of real friendship; it partly defines it.

Question: Whose opinions truly count? Answer: The opinions of those to whom we truly matter, and the opinions of those who truly matter to us. 'They know me', I will say, when the chips are down, the sand has run through, the excrement has hit the fan (and we have run out of metaphors). They know me, and therefore I am content that they judge me. 'Truthful and tender', as Emerson said. This is how our friends put us at our ease.

We are lovingly, mercifully, deeply assessed and professed by our friends. They thus serve as icons of God. Is this what the French philosopher Simone Weil means, when she writes that 'nothing among human things has such power to keep our gaze fixed ever more intensely upon God, than friendship for the friends of God'? Is this why we dare to sing the hymn:

> Thy mercies how tender, how firm to the end!
> Our Maker, Defender, Redeemer and Friend.

5

The trials of a life

———◆———

All wisdom must be paid for with pain.
Welsh proverb

I see that I must give what I most need.
Anne Michaels

In our life – which is, throughout, a form of journey or pilgrimage – we learn Christ at our own level, at our own pace and in our own way. We learn Christ on *our* everyday road, which is also his. As all roads are.

So we too move in and out of the wilderness; we too keep and lose friends. And in our own way, we too are on trial for our lives.

Trying too hard?

The verb 'to try' is interesting. It comes originally from a Middle English word meaning 'to separate' or 'distinguish'. In addition to its more usual meaning of attempting to do something, it has come to mean to *test* – especially by subjecting something to suffering or hard treatment – and so to investigate, experiment, settle, 'prove'; and also to purify. A 'trial' is a procedure that involves such testing or examination, a process that is a 'trying experience', which is another common meaning of the word.

I want to focus here on two of the ways in which we use this language. The first is judicial, denoting a courtroom investigation to settle a person's guilt or innocence, with evidence assessed,

witnesses tested and judgement decided. The second is more physical, even material. In this case we speak of a trial of strength that
taxes one's powers of endurance, or of a laboratory or industrial
process of refining or testing – perhaps, as in the engineering lab,
a 'testing to destruction'.

Religion has applied both usages, as metaphors, to our everyday
life. Hence life has been seen as a place of judgement and as the
location where the verdict of that judgement is carried out. But life
has also been understood as a furnace, forge or refinery: a place
where we pass through trials so that we may be strengthened and
our impurities burned out.

Is there anything to be said for either view?

Where's the justice?

A couple of centuries ago people used to speak more readily about
God's 'moral providence' in this world. By way of illustration they
pointed to the swift retribution that often falls on the malefactor,
quite apart from the intervention of human law. In our day such claims
are usually much more muted, but some religious extremists have
spoken of HIV as an instrument of God's justice; and if the wind
is in the right direction, you can sometimes overhear spiritually
arrogant businessmen claiming that their financial success is a consequence of God's benevolence, bestowed as a reward for their piety.

The Old Testament offers plenty of material to encourage this
view. The people of Israel and their monarchs are often routinely
described as flourishing or being brought low depending on their moral
or ritual piety. For example, in the books of Kings one monarch after
another is declared a sinner ('he did what was evil in the sight of the
LORD') and shortly afterwards the text reports that God's wrath was
exercised against him, usually expressed through a life cut short by
his enemies (see, for instance, 2 Kings 13; 16). By contrast, a small
minority of the nation's rulers are blessed in this life for doing 'what
was pleasing' to God. The Psalmist takes up the underlying theme:

'I have been young, and now am old, yet I have not seen the right-eous forsaken' (Psalm 37.25).

Well, I have been young too, and even though I am now only in the second flush of late middle age (or thereabouts), I can report that I *have* seen the righteous get it in the neck. And more than once. I have also seen the world's bastards wax healthy and triumphant. And so have you. Indeed, as the saintly Job complains, they are more likely to flourish.

> How often is the lamp of the wicked put out?
> How often does calamity come upon them?
> (Job 21.17)

> Have you not asked those who travel the roads,
> and do you not accept their testimony,
> that the wicked are spared in the day of calamity,
> and are rescued in the day of wrath?
> (Job 21.29–30)

Quite so. No, this life is not modelled on a judicial examination, where the truth is always out and the come-uppances are justly distributed. 'It's not fair,' we wail, quite early on in life. If they are wise, our parents will at least sometimes reply, 'No one said that it would be.' Although this may be true, we still cannot stop ourselves *expecting* fairness, particularly if those who brought us up exerted an equitable discipline, and taught us that we ought to be fair to our brothers and friends – and even our sisters. Schools don't really help, either. The morally better the school – that is, the more fair and just is the micro-society it strives to create within its walls – the less, in a sense, does it prepare us for real life.

For Life, with a capital L, is not fair. It *ought* to be, certainly; but it isn't. Even when the race goes to the swift, the swift are never swift just by their own efforts. Their genes and environment, those twin reprobates that answer to the names of Nature and Nurture, play a large part as well; and *they* are distributed with little regard to our worthiness or the honesty of our toil, as we have seen in earlier chapters. In any case, the race of life does not always go to the swift. Random chance is sometimes the more powerful explanation of how things turn out. 'As luck would have it, Providence was on my side', to quote the words of Samuel Butler's hero in *Erewhon*.

Let us not pretend, then, that this life is just. Quite apart from any human intervention, the way the world goes is *a*moral, non-moral. That is the nature of worlds. They are complex lumpy things, convoluted networks of causes and effects that are in themselves utterly impersonal and beyond morality. 'What have I done to deserve this?' people ask, faced with the birth of a handicapped child or the death of a lover too young to die, or the onset of their own terminal illness. It is not true to say that there is no answer to that question. There is this answer: 'You have done nothing; it is not a question of deserving.' Weal and woe, pain and fortune, dearth and death are distributed by the natural processes of this world gratuitously, indiscriminately. Who will dare to say that they are not?

But in a recent conversation with someone who had had a leg amputated, I was reminded that there are those who still deny the randomness of suffering. This man had been quizzed by a hospital chaplain, who asked him, 'Why do you think this happened to you?'

The unfortunate patient answered, as he should, 'Well, these things happen. It was just chance.'

'No', retorted the clergyman. 'There must be a more particular reason; something to do with you.'

The remark was possibly intended only to evoke some positive reflection in the patient as to how he should view his disability now – as a personal challenge, say. But it sounded to him, as it sounds to me, more like the old claim that we deserve to be blamed for our own suffering.

Out of court

Despite Job's urging and Israel's sorry history of the murder of God's prophets (see Jeremiah 2.30b), the Bible took quite a time to achieve the insight that we are *not* to blame for our suffering. It got there eventually, however. A man born blind stumbles by and the question on everyone's lips is, 'Rabbi, who sinned, this man or his parents?' The answer from the Jesus of John's Gospel is 'Neither' (John 9.2–3). A tower collapses and 18 innocents die. 'Do you think that they were worse offenders than all the others living in Jerusalem?' Jesus asks. 'No, I tell you' (Luke 13.4–5). After all, does not God send his sun and his rain without discrimination, on the evil and the good alike (cf. Matthew 5.45)?

Such words are quickly forgotten, however. And, to be frank, the New Testament itself equivocates on the relationship between sin and suffering, the alternative view being available to those who still seek it in 1 Corinthians 11.30 and James 5.15–16, perhaps even in Mark 2.1–12. Some may be relieved to learn this. We seem to find it natural to blame people for the evils that befall them. In 1703 a great storm swept across England, killing eight thousand people. It was interpreted as God's punishment on the nation, and a day of fasting was called when prayers for forgiveness were earnestly intoned. Doubtless people disagreed as to the particular sin that had provoked the Almighty's wrath on this occasion (Daniel Defoe apparently thought that the storm was a judgement on political disagreements). But probably most would have agreed that there must have been *something*.

This is only one example of the way in which Christians, ignoring the lead – or at least the strong hints – offered by Jesus himself, have assumed that this life is a trial of justice, a place where punishment is meted out for my sins or for someone else's sins. The traditional candidates for the role of 'someone else' have been Adam and Satan. In the case of the first nominee, it was often said that we suffer because we share a guilt for Adam's first sin, and are being punished in this world for that primordial crime of disobedience against God. In the second case, it was thought that God respected so much the freedom of the Devil and his followers that, rather than limiting their supernatural power, they have been given leave to torment us with disease and suffering.

Put baldly like that, these theologies seem worse than absurd. How can God be defended in the face of such bizarre claims? I call them bizarre not so much in acknowledgement of our doubts about the existence of a historical Adam or a supernatural Satan, as because of the *moral* difficulty of justifying such behaviour on the part of God. A God who behaved like that would not be showing justice at all.

Test-tube baddies

So much for life as a judicial trial and a place of just punishment. What of the alternative interpretation: life as a testing, proving furnace – a trial of our moral and spiritual strength? This account views life, in John Keats' famous phrase, as a 'vale of soul-making'; in the Psalmist's words, it is a life in which we are tried 'as silver is tried' (Psalm 66.10).

At first sight this second understanding seems as bad as the other one. It suggests, after all, that suffering, danger and hardship are planned by God – injected into the world to firm up the muscles of our character. It puts us in mind of stereotypes of the old-fashioned boarding-school housemaster or National Service drill-sergeant, laying on cold showers, warm beatings and wet cross-country runs in order to 'do us good'. Even worse, it implies that we ought to be grateful for these allotted trials, mouthing the mantra of the gymnast and the politician the world over: 'If it's not hurting, it's not working.'

Yet at least one theologian has encouraged us to take this vale of soul-making stuff seriously. Imagine, he suggests, the alternative to a world of woe: a struggle-free world without any pain or suffering. Our initial reaction may be that that sounds just perfect, thank you – this idea of a state in which everything in the garden is, and ever remains, lovely. According to John Hick's theology, however, the catch in the scenario is that such a painless world would be without compassion and courage, since these virtues would simply not be required of us in a place like that. No suffering, no compassion; no risks, no courage.

There would be nothing to avoid and nothing to seek; no occasion for co-operation or mutual help . . . The race would consist of feckless Adams and Eves, harmless and innocent, but devoid of positive character and without the dignity of real responsibilities, tasks, and achievements. By eliminating the problems and hardships of an objective environment, with its own laws, life would become like a reverie in which, delightfully but aimlessly, we should float and drift at ease.

The vale of soul-making perspective identifies our testing and often dangerous environment as precisely the sort of world that is required for our moral and spiritual growth. This world is a hard place to grow up in, but perhaps it is the best sort of world for the development of the human spirit. Hick argues that 'there could not be a person-making world devoid of what we call evil'. But he has also admitted that his wider argument invokes a value judgement, 'that one who has attained to goodness by meeting and eventually mastering temptations . . . is good in a richer and more valuable sense' than a person who was simply created virtuous 'all at once'. Having everyone born good and brimming over with compassion would conceivably make for a nicer world, but not a *better* one. Character is best forged in the furnace.

This account of the way things are offers some sort of explanation of the distribution of the world's suffering. Human suffering has to be distributed randomly, because otherwise it would not serve its soul-making function; suffering must be a mystery, because a non-mysterious distribution of trials simply would not work. The reasoning goes like this. If the sufferer's pain were clearly for her ultimate good (or indeed, as in the earlier view, a part of a deserved punishment), it would evoke neither our sympathy nor our aid. We would not then join the battle against evil. But some would say that encouraging that battle is God's main reason for allowing a world that contains evil in the first place.

More generally, even if much of the evil in the world appears to be pointless, 'A world without it would be a world in which life would be unimaginably different.' This is how the sceptical philosopher Anthony O'Hear develops the point.

> Unless we are prepared to say that a world with no suffering and with all the loss of depth and potential for achievement that this would entail would be a better world, then we are in no position to assert categorically that a good and all-powerful God could not have made the world as it is . . . What I am certain of . . . is that many of the most noble, dignified and sympathetic of men's responses to the suffering and tragedy in existence are responses precisely to the apparent gratuity of it all.

Do we really want a world in which life is fair? Don Cupitt suggests not, for another reason. If Nature and morality were fully harmonized, he argues, not only would no one feel sorry for the sick or unfortunate, but 'the ruling class would be superbly, and justly, *self-righteous* to the highest degree'. Not a pleasant sight – and certainly not an edifying one.

Between two evils

Is life a courtroom or a school of virtue? I tend to think that the second option is the better alternative, if only because it finds a place both for the point and for the pointlessness of tribulation, and because this is the sort of trial that I might just be willing to accept. On this view of things, the key words are not 'justice' and 'punishment', but 'struggle', 'growth' and 'strengthening'.

There is a paradox, however, in this account. Evil is viewed here as something we need as a part of our life, if we are freely to develop a worthwhile moral and spiritual character – as opposed to our just surviving as God's pampered and protected pets. We are forced to admit, therefore, that struggle and suffering are intended, in the sense that this is how God intends the world to be. But we can only interpret this as God's general intention, or else the requisite mystery would vanish. We cannot say that God intends this particular trial or that particular pain; we cannot look on any given unit of suffering as deliberately planned. For if we were to do so, the point of its pointlessness would disappear. Our religious response depends on 'the apparent gratuity' of suffering, on its very injustice.

Of course, much of the pain of our world is an inevitable part of the nature of Nature, a consequence of God's decision to create a *physical* universe at all. A physical world is necessarily imperfect, tending to disorder and decay; and any life that evolves within it will share these characteristics. It will be fragile and mortal. Further, in a world of matter, whenever objects come to occupy the same space at the same time as other objects, collisions and compressions are bound to occur. If sentient (feeling) creatures are involved, this leads to pain and possibly a hostile reaction. It doesn't matter if unfeeling stars collide; but when the fungus invades your foot, the snake bites your heel or the cancerous cells spread within your lung, your pain receptors will fire. They evolved for a good purpose, to make us aware of and so capable of avoiding dangerous situations in the outer world (such as snakes); but conflicts within our bodies produce the same effects.

Some prefer to say that God does not intend cancer or earthquakes (or biting snakes?); that they are – in the theologian Keith Ward's words – just 'necessary consequences . . . of the order of Nature'. In order to avoid all such suffering, one of two divine options would have had to be adopted. On the one hand, God might have created only immaterial minds ('spirits') that do not occupy space. This is the traditional understanding of the nature of angels. But we aren't angels. In restricting creation in this way, God would not have created us or our world.

On the other hand, God might continually step into the natural order to prevent our suffering; or providentially steer Nature away from any chance of hurting us. But then, either there would be no real material 'world' at all, nothing with any intrinsic structure or order about it; or the only available environment would be without risk or need, and therefore (as we have seen) would not promote moral maturity.

These were not God's intentions. He intended us in this world, as physical creatures that are inevitably vulnerable to occasions of pain and suffering, many of them inescapable.

But God also intends that we should resist them. We ought to look at this second claim more closely. All agree that Jesus was a healer of people's bodies and minds. In the Gospels he wages an unremitting war against the 'powers of darkness', including physical and mental illness. It is a conflict that he called others to join. Unless we resist evil, this approach argues, we will not become the sort of people that God intends us to be. We can only triumph over suffering, we can only be tempered in its furnace, *as we fight it*.

So the truth about suffering is to be found on two levels. God intends the evil (at one level – the general level) that he also intends (at another level) that we should work to destroy.

Where is the hand of God in this? It is necessarily hidden. T. S. Eliot famously echoes this theme:

> Who then devised the torment? Love.
> Love is the unfamiliar Name
> Behind the hands that wove
> The intolerable shirt of flame
> Which human power cannot remove.

If love is behind our suffering, then it is a long way behind. That is how we must think of God's involvement in the structures of a natural world that constrains, pains and shortens our lives. 'If God watches the sparrow fall', the American theologian Holmes Rolston comments, 'God must do so from a great distance' (see Matthew 10.29). For our sake, love cannot – love must not – become visible in the flames; else we should not strive to douse them. And it is our striving that God seeks, rather than our burning.

Several points follow from this. First, it means that there is a proper spirituality of fighting 'natural evil' (that is, suffering inevitably caused by an ordered but precarious physical Nature, including disasters, droughts and diseases). We should resist this testing; we should not go 'gentle into that good night'. The theologian Daniel Migliore calls this our 'faithful resistance', 'our courageous resistance to evil'. We may think of it as the proper work of His Majesty's Loyal Opposition.

Yet, second (as we saw in Chapter 3), there is also beyond this a proper spirituality of acceptance – in this case of accepting suffering and death. This involves discerning the hand of love in it, embracing – with St Francis – 'Brother Fire' and 'Brother Death'. It includes our grateful acceptance of our finitude as we concede, in the words of the Protestant theologian Karl Barth, that even 'our perishing, the termination of our existence . . . is the good order of God.'

Harry Williams has written of an *active acceptance* that transforms suffering. He maintains that it is the fruit of 'the mysterious giving of life', which is one of the forms of love. Is this why all 'prayers of asking' seem ultimately to reduce to the petition that Jesus himself prayed, 'Your will be done' (Matthew 6.10; Luke 22.42)? Dewi Phillips, the Welsh philosopher of religion, suggests as much:

Medical treatment has failed, and a child is dying.

Religious parents pray, 'O God, let her live.' What does this amount to? The parents recognise that things can go either way; the child may live or it may die . . . But they meet the possibility of things going either way in God. They recognise their own helplessness, that the way things go is beyond their control, and seek something to sustain them which does not depend on the way things go, namely, the love of God.

Cupitt makes an even more radical case for what he calls a 'strange new way of tackling the problem of evil'. 'Accept and endure it all, without a murmur of complaint. We overcome evil when we do not let it drive us into bitterness or resentment; the true conquest of evil is simply magnanimity.'

Third, there is a spirituality of times and seasons. What I mean by this is that there is a spiritual wisdom that tells us when we must resist and when we need to surrender. Learning that sort of wisdom is possibly the hardest part of the trial of our life. I do not doubt that it may be a spiritual mistake, as well as a medical and psychological mistake, to give in too soon. But it is plainly a spiritual mistake to fight to the *bitter* end.

Finally, however, I must add this comment. I do not think that we dare believe any of this of anyone but ourselves. This is *our* story. It cannot really serve as an 'explanation' to foist on others, nor even some species of spiritual whistling in the dark that we can offer to comfort them. It is too personal and too fearsome for that. Maybe we cannot *seek* it even for ourselves. As Phillips also says, 'It seems to be both a logical and moral truth that to seek one's character development is to lose it'; adding that we must beware 'an indulgent concern with oneself'. Perhaps, then, we can only pray, in words that express what is probably the original meaning of the petition at the end of the Lord's Prayer, that we may in the end be spared. 'Father, preserve us from the time of trial.' Keep us from being put to the last great test. But if it comes, let it not destroy us.

The theology of soul-making is not to be thought of as objectively testable. If it were, it would surely fail. More souls are broken on the wheel of life than turn with it, insofar as we can assess. But theologies are not based on quantifiable assessments. This one isn't, anyway. It is more like a lens through which we try to see our own lives. Through this lens our suffering could look strangely different, and that may contribute to our healing. Could this be part of what is meant by a gaining of a life that appears to everyone else to be a losing of it (cf. Mark 8.34–35)? It surely sometimes seems like a loss to us as well, when we can no longer focus through the glass. So as we pray for strength, we pray for a sustaining vision. For what other strength is there that is always available to us, than that which comes from seeing things through the refractive power of the concept of God?

It must also be pointed out that this is a present-tense sort of answer – or, better, a response – to evil. It needs to be. We are contrary creatures. Tell us there is something else coming if we will only endure this, and we might wait for ever for the something else but miss the point of the enduring (and the point of the 'this'). When religious blessings are presented as a reward or a future reversal of this temporal trial – that is, as 'something else' – we shall be tempted to look beyond the trial and not *through* it. But often the blessing is a part of the trial, an aspect of it. It is a different way of seeing the same thing; it is another evaluation, a different vision. 'Speak to me *beyond* this pain,' Job cries to his God, or so we may paraphrase him. 'Let it end, and then please explain what it has all been about. Tell me where you are and why you did this.' But when the Lord answers from out of the vortex he says nothing worth hearing except the un-spoken message, 'I am already here.'

If only I can get through this painful relationship, this bitter experi-ence of failure, this physical torment or this period of depression, *then* I shall be healed. Or so we often feel. But Paul writes, '*Now* is the acceptable time . . . now is the day of salvation' (2 Corinthians 6.2). The cross is *already* our victory; the widow has already given more than the millionaire; the little child does not need to become somebody in order to be somebody. Having nothing, we yet possess everything. Dying, behold we live (2 Corinthians 6.9–10). The trick, once again, lies in the seeing.

If we will allow the Christian gospel to say anything to our lives, we must allow it to speak in this still small voice about the present, even about the sufferings of the present. We should not be too anxious about what is to come. Things may get better or they may get worse. We must mind only this: that our present experience of hell may already be a sort of heaven, and our sorrow a type of joy.

Meaning what?

Does this imply that the trials of our life are somehow 'meant'?

I shy away from that word, because it easily leads on to the same slippery slope of spiritual despair and inhumane theology that I crit-icized earlier. That is where the hospital chaplain's question pushed the man whose leg has been amputated. Yet I am willing to allow that our sufferings can be said to 'have meaning' and to be 'meaningful', implying by these words that they can form part of a spiritual viewpoint that is able to sustain and heal us. For then our pain may seem, at least in retrospect, to have an odd sort of *value.*

I assure you that these are not the words of a hero or a masochist. As yet I have suffered comparatively little, as suffering goes; but I still wish that I had suffered less, and I have no wish at all to suffer more. Sporadic broken relationships and tooth abscesses have been quite enough, thank you. Nonetheless, I have to acknowledge that, taken overall, success and comfort in life have taught me very little, whereas my failures and trials have taught me a great deal. I wish it were not so; but it is. The Greeks had a proverb for it: *pathei mathos*, 'through suffering comes learning'. At the back of every beautiful thing 'there's been some kind of pain', as Bob Dylan sings. The lovely times were lovely; I can say that without qualification. Nevertheless, I grew more during the hard seasons.

And when I look at others I think it is often true of them also. Each must judge for himself or herself in this matter; but isn't it true that, while those people who have experienced very little suffering can be a pleasure, that is often all they are? Whereas those who have suffered much have something more to offer. They have learned something more – sometimes, much more. They have a depth. They have learned Christ, on the ordinary way of the cross.

Christian pain

But is our painful learning always a learning of Christ?

Very often, of course, it is not. For example, there are those tooth abscesses; and the time when, at the age of 11, I learned how well metal conducts electricity. It was not in a science lesson, but when I tried to start a fire in the household grate without matches. I made a spill of paper and touched it against the radiant bar of an electric fire. Unfortunately, the paper was from a discarded pack of cigarettes and carried a metallic foil backing.

71

This shocking piece of education was a species of secular learning that resulted in a deeper knowledge of electrical conductivity. It certainly taught me a lesson that I have never forgotten. It was not, however, a piece of 'Christian learning'.

Kierkegaard writes of something more holy in his powerful book, *Training in Christianity*. 'To live here in this world, is to be put on trial,' he insists. 'It is an examination. And the greatest examination [one] has to take, an examination which involves one's whole life, is that of becoming and being a Christian.' Hence, 'to be a Christian is to believe in Christ and to suffer for the sake of this faith.'

For Kierkegaard, this means learning to know Christ 'in lowliness', in his 'humiliation', by striving to will The Good and to be The Truth.

Here a new dimension is added to the trial. Frankly, it is very hard to see the point of a great deal of physical pain. Mental and spiritual suffering, however, seems to fall into another category. This is particularly the case if it is not any old suffering, struggle or learning, but one in which sides are taken for or against a situation, for or against The Good. This is the sort of testing that really changes us, where the bearing or the fighting is for something beyond ourselves. In essence, such tribulation forms part of upholding a vision or keeping a good in place, and the wounds we receive under those circumstances are directly related to our concern for truth and bear witness to it.

It is in this context, I believe, that people most often confess that, although they may be cowed by the struggle, they have not been broken *spiritually* by it. We may hope that we shall survive our trials in this way, if and when the blows are rained upon us because we are protecting something good, something right – something of Christ.

Not all trials are like that, naturally; but some are and they may illuminate the others. Let us trust so. At any rate, we must allow that the struggle of living will seem to us most worthwhile, perhaps only worthwhile, when it bears witness to the truth that is Christ. For then the humiliation of our suffering can share something of the power and purpose of the humiliation of Christ.

'The purpose of the humiliation of Christ.' What is that, then? It is to reveal and express, in our gutter, the unqualified richness of the love of God. Therefore, Kierkegaard prays:

> Unto Thee, Lord Jesus Christ, will we pray that Thou wilt draw us entirely unto Thyself . . . If only Thou wilt draw us, then indeed all is won, even though, humanly speaking, we were to win nothing; and nothing is lost, even though, humanly speaking, we were to lose everything.

6

Bearing all for joy

———◆◆———

The best way of thanking God is to taste his goodness with all our palate
. . . God reads our hearts, and he knows whether we taste his kindness,
or not. Enjoyment is the sincerest thanks.

Austin Farrer

> O dying souls, behold your living spring;
> O dazzled eyes, behold your sun of grace;
> Dull ears, attend what word this Word doth bring;
> Up, heavy hearts, with joy your joy embrace.
> From death, from dark, from deafness, from despairs,
> This life, this light, this Word, this joy repairs.
>
> *Robert Southwell*

My title phrase, 'bearing all for joy', may serve us as a description
of many situations of everyday life. For the Christian it may also
evoke the image of Jesus at his trial, and of his bowing under the
yoke of the cross-beam that he dragged to the hill of his crucifixion.
Can that picture be applied to ourselves as well, as we do our
own cross-bearing after him, in order to be worthy of him, to be a
disciple (Matthew 10.38; Luke 14.27; Mark 10.39)? For 'the cross
always stands ready', as Thomas à Kempis wrote, 'and everywhere
awaits you . . . Turn above or below, outside you or within, and
everywhere you shall find the cross.' As disciples, followers and
learners we are called to bear in our lives the marks of the Master
(Galatians 6.17), 'carrying in the body the death of Jesus' (2
Corinthians 4.10).

74

And why? For *life*. 'So that the life of Jesus may also be made visible', and because 'those who lose their life for my sake will find it' (Matthew 10.39). And find not just life, not just any life – but a life of gladness, celebration, delight, enjoyment. 'Blessed are you when people revile you . . . on my account. Rejoice, and be glad' (Matthew 5.11–12a); 'You will have pain, but your pain will turn into joy' (John 16.20b); 'Looking to Jesus . . . who for the sake of the joy that was set before him endured the cross, disregarding its shame' (Hebrews 12.2).

'If you bear the cross gladly', Thomas à Kempis added, 'it shall bear you.'

Bearing up and down

'Bearing' has several senses, all of them related. It means to carry, to sustain, to strive or thrust; and therefore to produce or give birth to.

Giving birth is hell, as any father will recall. All those interminable hours with nothing to do in the labour ward. Or out of it – pacing the corridors dying for a smoke, even when you don't smoke. Sometimes mothers give the impression that it isn't that much fun for them either.

We don't know if Paul witnessed childbirth, but he keeps on referring to it. The Galatians are his children 'for whom I am again in the pain of childbirth until Christ is formed in you' (Galatians 4.19); and in his letter to the Romans he writes of the world in the travail of birth: 'the whole creation has been groaning in labour pains until now' (8.22).

What did Jesus know about the process? He speaks of a woman in labour as one who grieves, yet when she is delivered 'she no longer remembers the anguish because of the joy of having brought a human being into the world' (John 16.21). (And there must be something in that, or no woman would ever have more than one child.) Bearing all, then, *for joy*. The French poet Guillaume wrote, 'Joy always came after pain.' And that, we feel, is how it should be.

Joy-spotting

When I was a curate my vicar left most of my training to his slightly less junior curate; but he did offer me two pieces of advice. One was how to buy books for the parish bookstall. (Yes, really: 'First go round the shelves in the bookshop and choose what you want, then take them to the counter . . .') The other was more theologically profound. 'Jeff, you are quite good at expressing the pain of life and the struggle of religion, but less convincing at communicating its joys.' A fair cop, that one.

Some of us are by nature closer to trials than joys, recognizing them more quickly and dwelling on them for longer. For the luckier ones, this order is reversed. A Church that included both psychological types would not be a bad idea, then (so make sure you find one). But, spiritually speaking, it would be an even better idea to combine the two in one person, and in one place.

This, I suppose, is Harry Williams' idea of Lent as Easter-in-disguise (see p. 40). Childbirth too is not just about putting up with it for the sake of the result; since childbirth does not just involve bearing the pain but *bearing down* in the pain – and through it – because there is no other way out, for the mother or for the child, short of a Caesarean section. As we well know, and as I argued in the last chapter, there are some things that we need and desire that will come only through pain and trial. Some joys also . . .

One hardly dares speak of joy at the foot of the cross. But that too is a place for a sort of birth, for the creation of a new sort of existence. The Jews spoke at the time of the expected 'messianic woes', tribulations that were to mark the birth-pangs of the New Age. On the cross, Christians believe, Jesus incarnates – that is, he enfleshes – them.

It is a commonplace that the crucifixion of Jesus is not treated by the New Testament as a failure, a defeat that God needed to reverse by a resurrection. Rather, it is itself a victory. Jesus bears the enmity of the best religion, the most powerful state and the most perfect legal system that were available at the time. In that way, if no other, he 'bears the sin of the world'. And he conquers them. This degrading, tortured death, whatever it looks like to those who do not have the eyes of faith, is already a victory. He has borne the hatred, the carelessness, the sin; and thus he reigns from the tree. In the end, all evil has to be borne. Despite the cries of Passiontide – 'Remove this cup from me', 'My God, my God, why have you forsaken me?' (Mark 14.36; 15.34) – the evil is borne. And so it is absorbed. Quenched.

To call the cross a victory over sin and suffering – a victory that brings God close to us – is to have come to learn what 'victory' is. It is to have come to see what 'power' is; what 'success' is. And therefore who God is. 'When the centurion, who stood facing him, saw that in this way he breathed his last, he said, "Truly this man was God's Son!"' (Mark 15.39). This is faith, which is a form of salvation, as a response to the bearing of evil.

It is very difficult to make sense of any of this. Let's not pretend otherwise. Why did Jesus die like that? Indeed, why does the New Testament claim that 'it was necessary' for him to die at all? All I want to say here is that it must have something to do with *bearing*, and that bearing is another of those everyday experiences that make and transform our lives. We do know something about this.

But here I go again, banging on about pain when I am supposed to be striking a lighter note in this chapter. Something about joy, wasn't it?

Joyriding

Robert Solomon's book *The Passions* contains a long chapter that serves as a sort of natural history of the emotions. If we use it to look up 'joy', we discover that he labels it a mood. Moods, unlike emotions proper, do not have a particular focus or object, in the way that (say) anger normally does. A mood, rather, is 'cosmic in scope'; it is directed to 'Everything'. However, moods are constructed upon the base of particular emotions and these remain within them, deep-down at their core. Such emotions function like a 'precipitating particle that crystallizes the mood', Solomon writes, remembering his chemistry. And joy is a mood that often centres 'on a core of delight'.

'Joy' is a fine word, as is 'delight'; they label glorious dispositions of the spirit. In Solomon's account, joy is 'that happy passion that renders our world . . . "wonderful", "marvellous".' We are indeed deeply blessed when we feel joy.

But can we really do so at the cross? Can there be joy and marvelling there? However keen we may be to move on to the taste and sources of joy, the cross still gets in the way. We cannot ignore the paradox of this conjunction of joy and crucifixion. Yet Christians do rejoice in the cross. They are glad of it; they delight in it; they celebrate it. How can the cross teach us anything about joy?

An ancient Latin verse, from the Roman Missal's *Exsultet* for the evening before Easter, begins '*O felix culpa*'. It describes the sin of Adam in terms that are thoroughly paradoxical: 'O happy fault, which merited such and so great a Redeemer'. Even for those (including me) who do not believe that there ever was a historical Adam, this can still be a potent and authentic image. That's worth pondering for a moment. It is just not true that Christianity cannot survive the withering fire that explodes old theological interpretations and precritical historical claims. Rational criticism may inflict terminal wounds on many of our beliefs about God, the world and history; but the depth and heart of religion still seem to survive intact. They do for me, anyway. The pattern of the Christian drama, expressed in the Easter liturgy and the traditional Nine Lessons and Carols at Christmas, may heap legend on myth, but I cannot help finding it deeply, movingly true. In their references to Adam they still say something powerful.

Their message is this. The first and so the worst sin, the foremost sin, has become the occasion of the pre-eminent salvation. The rebellion has been turned; the forces of darkness disarmed. The crib is the first location for this change, but its full power and manifestation was yet to come. The cross is supremely the place of reversal. It is the site where life comes through death, and victory through defeat.

It is also, therefore, the place where joy comes, through and in desolation. The beautiful phrase, the 'fullness of joy', marks both the 'path of life' and the presence of God in Psalm 16 (v. 11). Can it be applied to the cross? The claim that it can is all of a piece with much of the best religious thinking about joy – and with our own day-to-day experience as well. Here, I believe, is another truth that we have felt.

We know from our ordinary lives that there is a special quality and quantity of joy that is to be found in the most unlikely places. It is there in the mean and the mucky, in the transient, in the plain naturalness of Nature, and in the grubby faces of our neighbours. If these situations do not have for us the status of the holy emblem of the cross, it is possibly because we have forgotten what a mean, low, unprepossessing, ten-a-penny, squalid, temporary structure a real cross actually is. The cross is significant as the mode of Christ's death not because it is a permanent, glorious or worthy type of place; but because it isn't. If we can learn to rejoice in the cross, then, we might be able to rejoice at and in even smaller things. And vice versa.

So let us reflect on the joy of some little things; let us rejoice (as John Barton has written) 'in the world, in our daily lives, in the unspectacular satisfactoriness of just being'.

The transitory

Don Cupitt is still perhaps the religious thinker that most religious thinkers love to hate. But, as I have already hinted more than once, he has never been more than partly wrong. Cupitt is right about a great deal.

He is right, for example, in condemning the self-serving and self-interest that often masquerade as religion, as they often masquerade as love. He is right about the centrality of the ethical in Christianity, and in his claim that we should not understand this in terms of saving our own souls unspotted from the world but as a matter of burning ourselves out for others, as the sun does. (He calls this 'solar living' and 'solar ethics', and describes it as a matter of living a 'dying life' – 'because the self becomes itself only in passing'.) In particular, I believe, he is right about our need to love life and to embrace the everyday 'precious ephemerality of everything'. The literal meaning of the word ephemeral is 'lasting only a day'.

In his book *The Time Being*, Cupitt writes of the 'necessity of ephemerality, life's urgent transience'. Cupitt's notoriety results from his radical orientation towards the ephemeral in *all* aspects of the religious quest – his turn 'to the fleeting, from eternity to time, from the long-term to the short-term'. We do not need to follow Cupitt too far along his radical route, however, to welcome many aspects of this shift of direction for spirituality and theology. Religion usually encourages us to take the diametrically opposite road, away from the world to an unchanging God, soul and heaven that subsist outside time. 'Change and decay in all around I see; O Thou, who changest not, abide with me.' Yet the Bible has actually got much more to say about God's presence in and through change and time. In particular, it tells of the role of God in the events of the salvation history of Israel, and supremely in the life and death of Jesus of Nazareth and the struggles and fulfilments of discipleship.

This is welcome. Indeed it is good news, for it is continuous with the secular history of our lives where comfort and strength come to us primarily through our experience of the presence of people and things in our time. It is in our ordinary lives that we most clearly become aware of our religious lives.

The natural world

Nature has traditionally been understood as the expressive end-product of God's creative will, and therefore as a form of revelation. We need to take this insight seriously.

Cupitt writes elsewhere of a type of almost mystical ecstasy – certainly a form of joy and delight – that comes from our immersion in the flux of Nature. He argues that our human rivenness can lead to redemption through what he calls 'ecstatic immanence', which he describes as 'an intense and joyous response to the pure flux of existence'. This is a species of rapture that drains us of our painful ambivalent feelings towards the world and other people, as we are melted by perception or empty ourselves in our human creations – even as they slip away.

The novelist and philosopher Iris Murdoch has written in a similar vein of our experience of Nature, in its beauty and otherness, as an occasion for 'unselfing'.

> I am looking out of my window in an anxious and resentful state of mind . . . Then suddenly I observe a hovering kestrel. In a moment everything is altered. The brooding self with its hurt vanity has disappeared. There is nothing now but kestrel.

As we succumb to such a moment, 'we take a self-forgetful pleasure in the sheer alien pointless independent existence' of Nature. Murdoch is writing here of overcoming a mood of self-preoccupation and self-concern (she is pictured brooding, as academics and writers will, on 'some damage done to my prestige'), and doing this by means of a letting go or transcendence of the self and its interests, which takes us beyond our own 'fat relentless ego'.

Most of us need this sort of focus on what is other than ourselves from time to time, for – as Dykstra puts it – 'virtually every personal and social evil has its roots in our need to manipulate the world into paying attention to us'. 'Look at me', I scream at a world that is intent on turning the other way. 'Pay some attention to me.' But the kestrel is very obviously *not* us, and not even remotely interested in us. Amazingly, that is the reason why it can save us from ourselves.

Our joyful experience of Nature is, or at least it can be, a healing. It is therefore not childish of people to feel closest to God in a garden, or in my case – feeling too ill at ease among the un(in)tended weeds of my own flower beds – on a hillside or by the sea. Professional Christians often treat such protestations as poor excuses for our not being in church. They ought not to judge so harshly or so superficially. For many people there is an at-home-ness in the natural world that they rarely sense in a church. This runs very deep, carrying overtones of our evolutionary origins. After all, Nature is the place we have evolved to fit – and to fit in. The renowned biologist Edward O. Wilson has coined the term 'biophilia' for this innate need to interact with the living world of which we are a part.

Putting the matter personally, I have many times plodded through the Cheviot hills among the Cheviot sheep, and felt, 'I could die here now, and be content.' Others will find that sort of at-home-ness elsewhere, of course; the secret is to discover where you feel most at home. (We cannot all snuff it in north Northumberland; it would be grossly unfair on the National Park wardens.) An experience of this kind is not to be thought of as an escape, nor as some sort of extraordinary, mystical or out-of-the-body experience. It is not even, really, a 'timeless moment'. It usually comes as part of a walk, in a changing landscape. It is worldly and temporal, through and through. It is just ordinary and everyday.

And please do not misconstrue my talk of death here. It is because I feel so alive on those hills that I am most ready to die there. 'Joy', Dean Inge says somewhere, 'is the *triumph* of life.' So it can be precisely the location where death has no more dominion.

Nothing lasts

Cupitt (who in this respect is very unlike Iris Murdoch) wants to wean us away from any hint of the old Platonic prejudice against change. Plato insisted that this world is an inferior copy of what is really real. It is a charade, nothing more than a play acted out by shadows cast by cut-out models based on real people and things. For Plato those real things, the 'Ideas' or 'Forms', are elsewhere – in heaven, if you like. This influential tradition encourages us to concentrate on arm-chair reflection directed to the ideals of perfect goodness, beauty or even geometry, instead of getting stuck into the flawed natural world and our embodied fleshly lives. It can be very dismissive of works of art and human fictions that extol those ever-changing twin streams of passing events, our living and our world.

This Greek philosophical view, so different from the mainstream biblical understanding of Nature, got into Christianity by the back door – a type of subterfuge for which the Greeks were once famous. Christianity was (and is) often tempted by it, frequently succumbing so far as to adopt a philosophical theology of a changeless ('immutable') deity, and even speaking of an unfeeling ('impassible') God. It is not surprising, then, that much of our culture has developed a prejudice against Nature and the body, which is in the end a prejudice against life itself.

Biblical faith was not like this. The God of the Hebrews was always changing, even changing his mind (remember Abraham in Genesis 18, negotiating with God over the fate of Sodom). And yet this God could still be pictured as a Rock in the desert: as the One who can cast a cool, secure, reliable shadow, so that men and women may flourish despite the harsh, ever-moving, fiery light of the sun. The biblical insight expressed in this metaphor is that even in his change, and even in our change, such a God could be relied on. God's stability was a moral unchangeableness, a constancy of values. It was a God with this character who created this sort of world – a world that is all change and all-changing; all sweat, sex and struggle. And it is the same God who declares it good, declares *all of it* 'very good' (Genesis 1.31a), even in its flux and fluidity.

It is of the very essence of God to last for ever. So isn't it remarkable that God spends for ever creating things that come into being and pass away? Things like joy. It is not just Buddhism that cautions us against clinging on to things. This is pastoral and spiritual common sense. Cupitt puts it like this: 'Selflessly to love the transient and let it go: that is beatitude.' And like this: 'Go short-termist . . . love life in its very transience.'

Nothing lasts; only in fairy stories does everything come right and people live happily 'ever after'. In this world, assuredly, nothing lasts.

Not even religious and moral conversions are that total or complete. Consider Ebenezer Scrooge's conversion, presented in Dickens' tale as an overnight change that resulted in a brand new character. And ask yourself, What if the story had continued in the same detail a few chapters longer? What would Scrooge have been like next Christmas – and the year after? Would he still be just as completely converted; not even a little bit humbuggy? Not ever . . . ?

In our human experience nothing lasts, nothing totally lasts; and it doesn't in the end matter. And beyond? In the picture language of the Bible, heaven is a party, a feast. That tells us something. Parties might go on all night, but they cannot last a moment longer than dawn. I've never been to one of those all-night parties that concludes with a champagne breakfast after a punt down the river, or (in its economy version) with a tramp home in last night's glad rags against the tide of the next morning's grey commuters. I've never done it, but I've seen it done. It looked to me as if the party was definitely over. Our feasts would soon cease to be festive if they lasted for ever. So people sometimes say that heaven must really be outside time, beyond it.

But this life is not. Everything changes here, in God's creative flux. Therefore we had better 'seize the moment', as people also say. But we should not do this wantonly, but reverently; not grasping the moment tightly in response to our panicky realization that life is passing us by, but cupping it in our hands gently as we would a mayfly. And then letting go. Such beauty lives only for a moment or two, anyway. Living beauty is like that, whether it belongs to the damselfly or the damsel. Must we always be complaining that things do not last for ever?

Our joyful responses will not last either, for joy is often an unexpected and transient thing. C. S. Lewis, like Wordsworth before him, was 'surprised by joy'; and William Blake counsels us not to bind this passion to ourselves, but to kiss it 'as it flies'. It is exceedingly hard for us to accept that it is quality and not quantity that is the measure of the spiritual life. More than that – it is the only true measure of all life. (So what can you do for parents whose child has died, except mourn with them the death, and then – eventually – celebrate with them the life?)

Let us then rejoice in all short-lived things.

The little things

And let us rejoice in the small things of life. Harry Williams describes joy as a 'cognitive faculty'. It is, he writes, a 'way of seeing and knowing' that gives us eyes and understanding, and opens up the world to us. Thomas Traherne, the seventeenth-century mystical poet and Anglican cleric, describes magnificently the proper nature of this perception of worldly joy.

> Your enjoyment of the World is never right, till you so esteem it, that everything in it, is more your treasure than a Kings' exchequer full of Gold and Silver. And that exchequer yours also in its place and service. Can you take too much joy in your Father's works? He is Himself in everything. Some things are little on the outside, and rough and common, but I remember the time when the dust of the streets were as precious as Gold to my infant eyes, and now they are more precious to the eye of reason.

This too is a bit of heaven on earth – this street, this dust. The claim chimes in with William Blake's invitation, 'To see a World in a Grain of Sand and a Heaven in a Wild Flower, Hold Infinity in the palm of your hand and Eternity in an hour'. This is true celebration – the true celebration of things that will not last, things that are just ordinary, the little things of our everyday lives. 'Why, who makes much of a miracle?' asks Walt Whitman. 'As to me I know of nothing else but miracles . . . To me every hour of the light and dark is a miracle, Every cubic inch of space is a miracle.'

Astonishingly, some pages further on from the passage quoted above, Traherne writes of the cross in a similar vein:

The Cross is the abyss of wonders, the centre of desires, the school of virtues, the house of wisdom, the throne of love, the theatre of joys, and the place of sorrows; It is the root of happiness, and the gate of Heaven.

I repeat, it is hard to speak of joy at the cross; it has got to be hard to speak of it there. But was the Last Supper as doleful as we imagine? Was it not a celebration, a thanksgiving, a *eucharist*? The disciples had been taught to pray for the bread of life and for God's forgiveness, not as something in the future, but now – 'now already, here already, this day already', as the New Testament scholar Joachim Jeremias once put it. The Last Supper is set in this present salvation time. 'Now already' the disciples sit down to their own messianic banquet, the feast of the End Time come early. There they celebrate this body and this blood, these fragile things that are to be broken and spilled. Things that pass away. In the Jewish manner, Jesus brings together the little things of life (bread and wine, the staple of the Mediterranean peasant) with the little, commonplace actions of everyday life (eating and drinking), and thanks God over them.

This is what a sacrament is. It is to set aside something ordinary and to praise God over it. This is 'consecration' – 'setting apart as sacred'. It is not so much a technique for making something holy, as a way of attending to the ordinary and thereby discovering that it is already holy. In the Last Supper the little things are celebrated. Perhaps that is part of what allows the cross to which it points to become a 'theatre of joys'.

We too should rejoice over the little things.

The least of these

And lastly, of course, we must take joy in the little people.

That sounds more patronizing than it should; I trust that you will by now understand how I intend it. It is of the highest significance that we should celebrate and rejoice in each particular, individual human being. And, if I may put it like this, the more ordinary the better (yes, myself included).

There are many reasons why we ought so to do. One undeniable justification is provided by George Eliot, in the famous final paragraph of her masterpiece, the novel *Middlemarch*:

> The growing good of the world is partly dependent on unhistoric acts; and that things are not so ill with you and me as they might have been, is half owing to the number who lived faithfully a hidden life, and rest in unvisited tombs.

And here is a greater authority. As his disciples continue to jostle for status among themselves, Jesus stands a child before them, to show them what true discipleship should be like (Mark 9.33–37; Matthew 18.1–5). He did this not because children are 'trusting' or 'innocent'; and certainly not because they are virtuous or pious. He did it because this particular he or she was a *child* – and whatever their attitudes, values or beliefs, children have no status. In biblical times a child was regarded as even more lowly than a woman.

As I want to argue in more detail in Chapter 8, I believe that we should primarily celebrate Jesus as the one who comes among us and really serves (Luke 22.27). So the child is the model for the Christian as Jesus is, in his lowliness. In Christian imagery, Jesus is first the child, then the servant, then the crucified. Small roles; big production.

A recurrent theme throughout this book is that the very idea of a point-scoring scale of achievement of spiritual status should be incomprehensible to the disciples of Jesus. The great and terrible parable of the Last Judgement in Matthew 25 is about doing or not doing good to 'the least ones', 'the smallest', 'the insignificant ones'. To serve or not to serve them is to serve or not to serve Christ. There is no other measure.

And here Cupitt has something else to offer us. On his account, Christian ethics particularly involves 'revaluing and upgrading people and things that have become depreciated'. It is a question, he writes, of 'loving the worthless and neglected and raising their value-gradings'.

And *we* do this. We do this value-raising by means of our life and speech: by remaking the valuational attitudes, actions and language of our culture, both privately (at home, work or play) and more publicly and politically. For Cupitt, this is now a task that is all 'up to us'; but even for a more traditional theology, it is still *our job*. On either interpretation, this ethics is redemptive, for us as well as for others.

> The way to salvation is by actively striving to push up our values, and ennobling everything that is currently rated too low ... There is very often a strong case for valuing something or someone more highly, speaking of it more kindly, giving it a better name, and so coming to appreciate it more and treat it better. This enriches both the world and us.

We may allow – as Cupitt will not – that grace can assist us in this. But whether we tread this way with the help of God, or without any support beyond that of other people, this is the royal road to joy.

How is it best done? The Christian revalues the devalued – glorifying the despicable, enriching the world, creating new objects of moral concern – by metaphorically laying Christ's image over those whom the world has trash-canned, 'so that Christ imaginatively catalyses a change in the way we value that person. That is his redemptive work.'

I would sometimes play with this image when I lectured on Cupitt's theology. As a finale I would put up on the overhead projector a transparent image of this wickedly non-realist theologian. There was often an uneasiness in the lecture room at this juncture. I imagined that I could hear the subdued chorus of undergraduate mutterings of derision, mingled with the virile sound of ordinands rending their garments. Undeterred, I talked them through the account of how we change our perspective on others, as I have just outlined it. And as I did so I would put over the photograph of Don Cupitt another acetate tile, this one with an etching of the crucified Christ.

The result was one of those total silences that are rare in lectures (at least they are in my lectures), which are a sign that people are really listening. So I think they got the message. The point, as always, is for us to see things differently. In this case, it is to see the despised differently: by seeing the despicable in, through, and *as* Christ. Nothing could be more biblical.

That is my excuse for quoting my other favourite ending from the novel *Franny and Zooey*. Franny and Zooey are sister and brother. Years before they had been child stars on the radio together. Now Franny, depressed about her acting career, is listening to Zooey telling her over the phone of an event from their shared past on *Wise Child*.

> 'Anyway, I started bitching one night before the broadcast. Seymour'd told me to shine my shoes just as I was going out the door . . . I was furious. The studio audience were all morons, the announcer was a moron, the sponsors were morons, and I just damn well wasn't going to shine my shoes for them, I told Seymour.'

Seymour had told him to shine them anyway: to shine them 'for the Fat Lady'.

> 'I didn't know what the hell he was talking about . . . He never did tell me who the Fat Lady was, but I shined my shoes for the Fat Lady every time I ever went on the air again . . . I had her sitting on this porch all day, swatting flies, with her radio going full-blast from morning till night. I figured the heat was terrible, and she probably had cancer, and – I don't know. Anyway, it seemed goddam clear why Seymour wanted me to shine my shoes when I went on the air. It made *sense*' . . .
>
> 'He told me, too,' [Franny] said into the phone, 'He told me to be funny for the Fat Lady, once.'

Zooey interrupts:

'I don't care where an actor acts. It can be in summer stock, it can be over a radio, it can be over *tele*vision, it can be in a goddam Broadway theatre, complete with the most fashionable, most well-fed, most sunburned-looking audience you can imagine. But I'll tell you a terrible secret. Are you listening to me? *There isn't anyone out there who isn't Seymour's Fat Lady* ... There isn't anyone *any*where that isn't Seymour's Fat Lady. Don't you know that? ... *don't you know who that Fat Lady really is?* ... It's Christ Himself. Christ Himself, buddy.'

For joy, apparently, it was all that Franny could do to hold the phone, even with both hands.

7

Beginning at the end

———•◆•———

With ashes on our heads we sit alone;
  The grief of all the world is ours to bear,
  The holocaust of history we share
With all who hoped to sing but learnt to groan.

Like a volcanic mountain overhead
  God is too close for comfort, and his love,
  The light of heaven and earth, rains from above
A dreadful mercy that begets us dead.

The faith and hope and love in us are sound
  Though our souls be insane, our bodies dust;
Our feet are walking over holy ground
  But touch it no more than a luckless ghost:
Our only business here is to abound
  And what is truly good shall not be lost.

Gordon Jackson

In the last four chapters we have explored some of the key motifs of everyday life – isolation, friendship, suffering and joy. As they are integral to our human journey, we need to make some sort of spiritual sense of them. Although I used many Christian references and illustrations in these discussions, much of what I have written could be appropriated by people of other religious faiths – and some of it by those without any faith who yet seek a spiritual perspective on their lives.

It is time now, however, to address some more specifically Christian concerns, and in doing so to pick up themes from the first two chapters. I shall touch on the topics of spiritual vision and 'learning Christ' here, developing them further in Chapter 8. In this chapter I want mainly to explore the tension between depth and superficiality in the Christian response to the gospel, with particular reference to our understanding of Christianity's 'end' (a word that signifies both something's *conclusion* and its *purpose*).

Back to front?

Mostly, we learn Christ backwards. The American scholar John Knox once illustrated how, in the New Testament, where an appropriate background to Jesus' human ministry seemed to be called for, it was sometimes provided by a belief in his divine pre-existence. In particular, the author of John's Gospel will not lift the curtain on the ministry of Jesus before treating us to a 'prologue' (John 1.1–18). It is as if the producer of a play addresses the audience directly before the performance, saying in effect:

> In the drama you're about to see, you need to know that this Jesus character, who walks about doing good and teaching about the Kingdom, is the very self-expression of God himself, the instrument of creation, 'with God' from the start. He is 'The Word'. Remember that. Now please enjoy the play.

The prologue changes everything. You cannot now see the earthly Jesus without the added dimension of this heavenly claim.

But where does it come from, this stuff at the beginning? Doesn't it come from the end, from whatever powerful experiences the disciples had that made them proclaim, 'He is risen'? They came to see everything about Jesus backwards, through the lens of this experience of resurrection. And this applied not only to Jesus' life, but also to whatever came before that. So some of the first Christians came to believe that it was not possible that the one who was to 'rise' should not have first 'fallen' – that 'Love came down at Christmas', as the carol puts it. The resurrection had revealed a new dimension, Jesus' real position and purpose in relation to God, which changed their perception of everything that came before. In a way, it works like this for us too.

Funny stuff, though, this 'resurrection'. The very idea of it makes me uneasy and I'm not helped by talk of a pre-existent Christ, which is even more difficult to imagine. What do we really mean by Jesus 'coming down' to us? And why should we view his humiliation – especially his suffering and death – *through* his glory?

This is an odd perspective to adopt partly because, although the life and death of Jesus were public, the resurrection wasn't. We tend to forget that, and treat them both as events on the same plane: cause and effect, one thing leading to another. Yet isn't their relationship more like that between the two dimensions of a plane surface and the other, third dimension, of depth or height – as with the table image I played with in Chapter 2? In the plane of the world what follows after life is death, and after death dissolution – THE END. The resurrection is at right angles to this; it is something else – a New Life, THE BEGINNING. That is why some theologians say that the empty tomb simply isn't that important, because the story of the absent body is still within the historical story; it is not part of the new story about the new dimension. (In any case, arguing from emptiness is a risky business – too much like arguing from silence.)

Perhaps we may say that, whatever else it was and is, the resurrection represents the *depth* of the death of Christ – and perhaps, too, of his life and his ministry of humility.

Waiting for the resurrection

I don't know. But then religious ignorance may sometimes be more illuminating than religious knowledge . . .

A recent survey revealed that only two-thirds of British adults know 'what happened on Easter Day'. This situation will get worse. Biblical knowledge among schoolchildren is dwindling fast, and I have seen a figure of less than 10 per cent quoted for the proportion of pupils at secondary school who know the basics about the meaning of Easter. Fewer and fewer people know about the resurrection.

My own, more impressionistic, evidence goes back to the early 1970s, when I first saw George Stevens' film *The Greatest Story Ever Told* in a West Midlands cinema. It was not the greatest film ever made about Jesus (and proved to be a commercial failure), but it did manage to keep the patrons in their seats – at least as far as the crucifixion. Then, as Jesus died on the cross, the cinema began to empty. Row upon row of filmgoers seemed to take Jesus' words 'It is finished' rather literally and untheologically, stampeding out of the cinema to ensure they caught the last bus home and avoided the National Anthem, which in those days was still played at the end of performances.

As a consequence, it was left to a mere handful of us – presumably the mere handful who had read the book – to witness the resurrection.

I now understand that that is the way it has always been, whether in Staffordshire or Jerusalem. For the world, Jesus dies on the cross and that is that. His death is public, empirical and obvious. His resurrection, however, is not for the world; it is reserved for the disciples. So Jesus does not appear to the Jewish Council that 'tried' him or the Roman soldiers who tortured him, but only to his 'little ones' who followed him on the road. These are those who had truly learned Christ, and were therefore able to see him. The resurrection was a secret: only to be experienced behind closed doors or by a mist-shrouded lake, or at dusk on the road to Emmaus. Even Paul's reference to the occasion when Jesus 'appeared to more than five hundred' (1 Corinthians 15.6) labels an appearance to 'the brothers and sisters'. The Bible speaks of a public crucifixion, but a secret resurrection.

Why does Mark's Gospel end so abruptly? (Take a look for your-self.) Verses 9 to 20 of Mark 16 are a later addition; the most ancient manuscripts end, as do most of our modern translations, with the women running away from the tomb beside themselves with terror. 'They said nothing to anyone, for they were afraid.' That's hardly a suitable finale for Cecil B. DeMille, Franco Zeffirelli, Mel Gibson or any other film-maker. Most scholars don't believe that an original ending has been lost, but that the actual resurrection appearances of Jesus were deliberately kept secret. This mystery was not to be blazoned across the papyrus; it was too holy, too 'numinous' to be published abroad. The resurrection was too sacred for words.

The cinema-goers got it right, in a way. The crucifixion *was* THE END (the 'superficial' end?) of the Greatest Story. The resurrection was and remains a secret, because it is beyond the end. The resurrection never really works on film anyway, and I don't think it really works in the narrative of the Gospels. The reason, perhaps, is that the resurrection is the beginning of another story, a new type of story – or a new depth of story.

In this book, however, I am not supposed to be discussing such extraordinary things, but things closer to home. So here goes. Here is my attempt at a Christian spirituality of resurrection – one that is about us and our lives.

Everyday resurrection

As we follow Christ on the everyday road, we will learn some everyday things. And some of them will seem to be in another dimension or on a different plane, though they are located in the midst of the everyday. Undergoing these experiences is like taking off at right angles, or suddenly seeing what lies under the surface of something. And *sometimes* the contrast with the rest of our superficial, mundane life is so complete that we may think of them as another form of living. Religious folk then speak of 'grace' or 'miracle' – or 'resurrection'.

I hope you've felt something like that, at least once. I vividly recall situations in which someone I loved said or did something that evoked in me the deadening emotions of intense anger or self-pity, but before I could express 'what came naturally' I was lifted out of myself by a tidal wave of compassion, affection or forgiveness. It was a new lease of life.

We need to recognize death when we see it. But like the disciples at the tomb, we also need to believe in resurrection. And to believe in it even when we don't see it. 'Why do you look for the living among the dead?' ask the figures at the empty tomb in Luke's Gospel (Luke 24.5). 'He is not here,' says the young man sitting in the tomb in the Gospel of Mark. 'Do not be alarmed . . . he is going ahead of you' (Mark 16.6–7). This is the disciples' new perspective, their new life. Like the Kingdom, 'eternal life' refers not only to something beyond death, but to a new quality of life *now* (John 5.24; 6.53–54; 14.18–19; 17.3). A new depth to living. And we have felt it.

Resurrection is not another event in the old history of events, something that can be easily woven into or explained by the old pattern of the old life. 'Do not remember the former things, or consider the things of old. I am about to do a new thing; now it springs forth, do you not perceive it?' (Isaiah 43.18–19). To believe in resurrection – to see resurrection – we shall have to experience rebirth and renewal, the miracle of the new. This is the miracle of depth: the ordinary become extraordinary.

The re-creation that is resurrection is, for Christians, the last and final hope in the face of all human endings. It is already our story, if we have known it in our own prosaic lives. In experiencing old endings and new, half-believed beginnings, we see beneath the superficialities of living, and taste the deeper things – and the sharper taste of a new, 'arisen' life. And we come to know, in Eliot's phrase, that the end is the place 'where we start from'.

The new age and its relatives

I want to explore this theme now with reference to our public, social context. For our culture engages in a way of thinking which itself constitutes a type of new beginning and a new form of living. A sort of resurrection.

We're often told that we live at the end of one age and the beginning of another. Maybe people have always been told this. In the eighteenth century, the voices that proclaimed the so-called Enlightenment 'modernity' of their new age insisted that all knowledge and values were now to be seen from a universal, human, rational perspective. The 'new day dawning' for us today is often described as *post*modern. If the jargon is unfamiliar, please bear with me. In truth, it represents nothing more than a late edition of modernity, in which the older, rather solemn and grand search for one universal human Reason, and one big, capital-T Truth, has gone on holiday. It has donned its gaudy shirt and shorts, and become a lot more laid back. 'Postmodernity' now offers a permissive welcome to all our little-t human truths, in all their variety. This, it must be confessed, is a form of *relativism*, in which truth is defined in relative terms, as that which is true 'for us'. (You will have met the phrase, 'it's all relative'. You may use it yourself.)

The guardians of religion usually regard relativism as bad news; and rightly so, up to a point. Certainly, unqualified relativism that says that any claim to truth is just as good as any other is bad news all round – if not self-contradictory. (In what sense is it 'true'?) There is, however, a humble, qualified relativism that is as unavoidable as it is liberating. It arises from the recognition of the limitations of our human perspective. It is the acknowledgement that we are 'only human', even – especially – when we speak of the divine. In our search for truth we always strive to go beyond ourselves, and we may partly succeed. Nevertheless, we must remember that this striving begins with us and will always have to make sense to us.

Can this perspective form part of the stuff of the resurrection of religious faith? Does it allow us to talk religion, and to talk about God, in greater *depth*?

Let's go back much further, for these questions are not really new at all. Two thousand five hundred years ago, a certain Xenophanes of Colophon (lovely name!) criticized the way in which the Greek poet Homer wrote about the gods. He was too 'anthropomorphic'. In other words, he portrayed the gods in the form of human beings. But, Xenophanes spluttered, if cattle, or lions, or horses had hands, just like humans; if they could paint with their hands, and draw and thus create pictures then the horses in drawing their gods would draw horses; and cattle would give us pictures and statues of cattle; and therefore each would picture the gods to resemble their own constitution.

In place of such a childish relativism, he offered his own 'true' god, one who is – wait for it – 'totally vision; totally knowledge; totally hearing'.

But who can escape their own perspective? No one. In its turn (actually 250 years later) this superintellectual deity was mocked by another critic, who said: 'Xenophanes, semi-pretentious, made mincemeat of Homer's deceptions, fashioned a god, far from human, equal in all his relations, lacking in pain and in motion and better at thinking than thought.'

He *fashioned a god*. This puts in an extreme form a truth that would hardly need mentioning, except that it is anathema to some religious fundamentalists. *Our* perspective on God is not, and cannot be, a divine perspective. However highly we rate the Bible or the Church, or the authority of any religious scripture or tradition, most of us do not doubt that the final form and content of these sources were framed within the minds, and on the lips and writing implements, of human beings. That was where they became the raw material for 'theology' – which is at base simply 'God-talk', our reflective human talk about God. Our theology is *human*, because it is ours. This does not mean that it cannot also be 'divine', in the sense of giving an account of divine things and even by doing so with divine authority. But theology can only be divine in the way that something human can be divine. As in other areas of religion, 'we have this treasure in earthen vessels' (2 Corinthians 4.7a). (At least in the Authorized Version we do; later translations locate it, less poetically, inside 'clay jars'.) This seems to me to show a proper humility about holy things.

Part of the resurrection of our religious faith must involve recognizing the true status of its words, images, stories and ideas. Religion can so often die at the hands of the literal-minded, or those who insist on the 'inerrancy' of their scriptures. It can die there because it is starved of the rich human imagery and inventiveness that give religious depth to religious language, and which come from the same fragile source (our God-given human imagination) that gives depth to all our language.

According to Xenophanes, each animal would picture God to 'resemble their own constitution'. So fish would do theology rather differently from the way we do it. And why not? In Rupert Brooke's poem 'Heaven', pious fish hope for 'somewhere, beyond Space and Time' where there is 'wetter water, slimier slime':

And there (they trust) there swimmeth One
Who swam ere rivers were begun,
Immense, of fishy form and mind,
Squamous, omnipotent, and kind;
And under that Almighty Fin,
The littlest fish may enter in . . .

And in that Heaven of all their wish,
There shall be no more land, say fish.

A. D. Hope, by contrast, has articulated the religious life of *cats*.

'Twice this week a scrap with Rover;
Once, at least, we missed a rat;
And we *do* regret, Jehovah,
Having kittens in Your hat!

Sexual noises in the garden,
Smelly patches in the hall –
Hear us, Lord, absolve and pardon;
We are human after all!'

The God of Cats hears these prayers, and blesses his worshippers appropriately:

Home at last from work in Heaven,
This is all the rest God gets;
Gladly for one day in seven
He relaxes with His pets.

> Looking down He smiles and ponders,
> Thinks of something extra nice:
> From His beard, O joy, O wonders!
> Falls a shower of little mice.

Why not indeed? (Although in the theology of mice, the nature of the divine blessing would be pictured rather differently.)

We shouldn't treat this sort of thing as a put-down of religion or a piece of sentimental flippancy, but as an endorsement of the power of language to make the mystery of God *imaginable* – and as a gentle, necessary ribbing of those religious people who think that their own words can fully capture The Word. 'Human speech', wrote the novelist Gustave Flaubert, 'is like a cracked kettle on which we tap crude tunes for bears to dance to, while we long to make music that will melt the stars.' If we take that seriously we are bound to see Scripture very differently. We need not deny that 'the record of divine revelation' is more than human; we need to affirm that it is never less than human.

Most of us have always thought so, because we belong to our age; and this, possibly, is its most significant insight – how very human we are. And therefore how human our views are, even our views about God. So let's not be browbeaten by the fundamentalists. I fear they are often in danger of missing the point of religion, by missing the deepness of its language and its humanity – and therefore of its spirituality.

Owning up

There is another feature of our age that promises a resurrection for our faith. Nowadays we own up to having a human perspective on things much more readily and honestly than we used to do. We are conscious of the role of persons in selecting, creating and construing meaning, rather than just passively stumbling against it as it lies around 'out there'. To that extent, our age is more *person*-al. As we have seen, we have inherited a lot of this from the Enlightenment, but recently we have become more conscious of the variety of meanings that an ever-changing variety of people engender and encounter.

This makes our age personal in an even stronger sense. The meaning of our life is now something that we more clearly acknowledge to be ours. Nowadays, there are some things that you really have to believe and do for yourself. One of them is morality; another is religion. Life, truth and religion all have to make sense to us now, in our human particularity and uniqueness.

Here is Harry Williams again, reflecting 40 years on about an episode from his Christian ministry in the 1940s, when he faced what was even then (at least for Anglicans) a rather old-fashioned pastoral problem about the use of contraception. His comments capture the new spirit of our own age perfectly: 'Today I should take the view that if people are silly enough to allow their conduct to be dictated by a bunch of clergymen, then they deserve whatever comes to them.'

We were supposed to have grown up in this way back in the eighteenth century. But the demise of deference in our society has actually been quite a slow thing. Gradually, however, it has eroded away. We are now a lot less willing to take our systems of beliefs, and particularly our attitudes and values, from other people or institutions. Of course, we do still receive beliefs and values second-hand, particularly these days from the mass media; but we are mightily resistant to influence from those other quarters – and queens – that we have not ourselves chosen to rule over us. We are, if you like, switched on only by those pundits that we chose to switch on. This is how we operate these days, although admittedly we can take it too far. (Postmodernity, it is sometimes said, is when we treat everything like the telly.)

This is not a simplistic total relativism. It is simply an expression of the realization that *our judgement counts*. Indeed, of course, in the end this is the only judgement that can count, *for us*. Were you to convert to my viewpoint it will be because you have changed your mind or, to put it more arrogantly, because I have changed your mind. Anyway, yours is the mind that has to change.

It would be foolish to equate this truism with the claim that 'only my views count', or that I am (or we are) 'the measure of all things'. That interpretation is very widespread, in a variety of forms. Even the great Enlightenment philosopher Immanuel Kant argued that 'the Holy One of the gospel must first be compared with our ideal of moral perfection before we can recognise him to be such'. As Basil Mitchell rightly remarked, this is 'preposterous'.

> It is absurd to suppose that the fisherman of Galilee – when he made the confession: 'Thou art Christ, the Son of the Living God' – had compared Jesus with his ideal of moral perfection (just as it was before any encounter took place) and had satisfied himself that he had, so to speak, achieved the required standard. [Peter] had, of course, judged for himself, and in judging he exercised moral insight, but he could not himself have preached the Sermon on the Mount.

People's beliefs and standards must be their own beliefs and standards, if they are to exercise their own judgement. But this doesn't mean that they invented these ideas; only that they have now accepted them.

Right. And I agree with Leslie Houlden that 'it is hard to deny that Jesus should be the critic rather than the mere endorser of those who hold beliefs about him'. But these claims still allow that we must always and can only 'judge for ourselves'. No one can come to believe in different things (whether truths, facts, values, messiahs or gods) without those different things coming into and becoming part of his or her own belief system or point of view. And that movement cannot take place without their being assessed, at some point and to some degree, by the believer's existing beliefs – even as they change. For Jesus to be my critic, I have to *accept* his criticism. Such transformations can only work 'against a background of what is held constant', writes the philosopher John Cottingham, 'through an activation, and a deepening, of moral intuitions that are already there'. As I hinted in the Introduction, in these fields the best authorities are often those that tell us what we already know.

Beliefs are believed. They are owned. Now, more than ever before, we insist on our ownership. No Bible or Church or king or priest will take that responsibility from us. So this is *our age*. And it is a form of resurrection, of new life.

Can this new 'personal' (even 'subjective') perspective also be a part of our corporate resurrection, our new life 'in Christ'?

Resurrecting churches

The Church needs to understand the prevailing cultural and intellectual tenor of our age. It knows about it, of course, and in its way it responds to it. But this is too often in the abstract, and that is no longer enough. In order to respond properly, the Church will also need to respond concretely, which means that the Church will need to understand us also. The way that we feel about our beliefs – in particular, that these are *our* beliefs, 'so there' – implies that we must now be taken seriously. Yes, *us*: this many-headed, non-deferential, great unwashed people of God.

Death and resurrection are to be found in our age and thinking and culture. We may hope, therefore, that they may be found in our Church, which is of this age and culture and patterns of thought. The death and resurrection of culture and ideology has been a great wonder, as the authority of big ideas and powerful voices has died on us, and our own little ideas and our own quieter and discordant voices have burst from their graves. It is a wonder, almost a miracle. But the resurrection of the Church would be a greater one.

'Come on', more cynical readers may respond. 'What has the Church to do with resurrection?' Alas, it often seems to be the body that is most resistant to its own rebirth. Nevertheless, the record shows that resurrection came first to the Church and for the Church; indeed, in one sense the Church *is* resurrection. The body of Christ is broken and dies, and the body of Christ springs into life (1 Corinthians 12; Ephesians 4.11–16; Colossians 1.15–20, 24); Jesus breathes his last, and then he breathes his Spirit on and through his disciples (John 19.30; 20.22); he leaves, and the Church is created; 'Jesus foretold the Kingdom, and it was the Church that came.' Whatever else it thinks it is about, the Church should be about resurrection.

Where can we see that now? Structural changes might help; financial factors are relevant; liturgical revision is of value; some 'fresh expressions' of Church will, I hope, flourish. All these new gasps of breath are very welcome. But something more radical, something a lot deeper, is needed.

In order to rise to join the new age, the Church needs finally and explicitly to die to all its old fantasies about authority and status, its often sanctimonious image and rhetoric, and its urge towards a single, monochrome spirituality. Especially it must die to its desperate impulse to *control* people's faith and morals, their religion and lives. It has to let us go.

I love the Church (well, sometimes). But I am also very critical of the Church, and particularly critical of some of its ministers. Before I get carried away, I should remind myself that I am technically to be numbered among them. However, I often feel like a lay person; and I can become as irritated as anyone at the superficiality of what is offered by some clergy, and especially irritated by the condescension that frequently accompanies it.

I know that clergying is a difficult job. I know too that at least 60 per cent of its difficulty comes from having to climb over a barrier that exists for clergy just because they are clergy – the presupposition that they 'must be different'. This is really no one's fault, except in those cases where priests and ministers still enjoy living behind barriers and being perceived as superior in some way. Such pleasures are childish and rather pathetic; but I suppose they are trivial, forgivable sins.

But there is something else that is rather less easy to forgive. I know many wonderful ministers of the Christian gospel. But there are, I fear, others. I am not alone in feeling that some clergy and church leaders simply get in the way of our spiritual growth. They don't mean to, naturally; but they do. Clergy get in the way when they want their way to be my way, when they want me to adopt a way that they have mapped out for me. I am not saying that that can never work. It might. But usually it doesn't. What if I am not like them? What if I don't fit into their categories?

As I said at the beginning of this book, these reflections represent only my way of seeing things. But it is *a* way and, because it's mine, it is more important to me than any other way of seeing things – including that of any minister, priest, academic theologian or bishop. *Necessarily* it is more important. I can only be me. Even when I change, *I* am the one who changes.

I can only be me. And you can only be you. And it is surely time, at the beginning of its third millennium, for the Church to respect that simple truth.

There is, to put it bluntly, no reason (in the sense of no ulterior motivation) for you to go to or claim to belong to any church, unless you want to or need to. And in our day we shall only want to do that, and we shall only feel the need for it, if our personal viewpoints are taken seriously – if *our* depth is taken seriously. All of us, with all our differences. That is the only proper way for the Church to take itself seriously because, of course, either we constitute the Church or we are those it wants to 'bring in'. We require that our perspective be taken so seriously that the Church expresses, represents and feeds *our* concerns, *our* spirituality, *our* lives, *our* morality, *our* worship and *our* faith.

In this new age, if we are not listened to we shall simply not stick around. Notice how the faithful are already seeping away.

If I am to dare to talk of ends and beginnings, of deaths and resurrections in the Church, I must say this. The future of Christianity lies with lay people. In a sense, of course, it always did; but now that sense has come galloping to the fore. This isn't a result of a commitment to 'democracy' or 'egalitarianism', or some trendy vision of the 'People's Church'; nor is it based on any sophisticated philosophical, theological or political idea. It certainly isn't because we haven't got enough clergy. (We have quite enough clergy; but perhaps not enough who are willing to identify the Church's major asset as being its lay people, or to see their own ministry as one of empowering others.)

What I am referring to is just a *cultural* shift. It comes with education, or rather it comes with a certain sort of education; and it comes with socialization into a certain sort of culture. It comes through historical change. Wherever it originates, it is a genie that cannot be pushed back into the bottle. It is a truth abroad-in-the-world that all religious bodies must eventually face.

The truth is that the future is us. *We* are the new beginning. If there is to be a resurrection of the Church, it will have to be ours.

The elusiveness of Christianity

Actually, this truth came first with the gospel itself, with the old beginning. 'Who do *you* say that I am?' 'What then shall *we* do?' 'As for *you*, come follow me.' That is the authentic gospel. But the gospel, as always, is hard to find. The American theologian Terrence Tilley writes:

The life of faith is a life lived under the guidance of a Christian vision. The articulation of that vision and the practice of the faith may vary from time to time and place to place. Christians use *these* expressions and engage in *these* practices and avoid *those* expressions and practices. Yet none of these expressions and other practices are sufficient to express fully and completely the gift of God itself. They are expressions of that gift. That gift can be known through them if it can be known at all. The faith, then, is not reducible to any one articulation of the vision or any one way of practicing the faith.

Where is Christianity? In a sense, Christianity does not anywhere exist. I mean by this that Christianity is to be had in a pure form, in its deep form, only as gospel ('good news') in the proclamation of the Christ. This comes and passes on, like the wind. That which remains, that which we can see and hear and touch and taste, is nothing more than a *response* – the variety of human responses to that gospel. These are the faces of Christianity, the outward and visible signs of the (essentially unobservable) inner response to the gracious demand of the Kingdom of the Christ-like God.

Christianity *is* that demand and that grace. It finds expression in many forms, not only verbal and intellectual (as doctrines, stories, myths and parables), but also visual and tangible (images, icons and rituals, lives and deaths). But it necessarily transcends all of these, as the meaning of a story or an action is more than the words or bodily movements that express it.

Christianity is the deep meaning lying behind and within the preaching and living of the words and works of Christ. It cannot exist purely 'objectively' quite apart from the responses of those who find meaning in it, any more than a piece of music really exists when it isn't being played or heard. We cannot see the gospel as such; we cannot even hear the gospel. All that we can see and hear are words, actions and things that bear the gospel. And they themselves are just expressions of the gospel, reactions to it. They are not the gospel itself. Likewise, the whole of the concrete, manifest Church is never more than a change elicited by the gospel. Its thinking (beliefs) and its acting (its way of life) are second-order realities. And our judgement on them, our evaluation of them as 'Christian', must depend on how appropriate and obedient we deem them to be as responses to the gospel.

What I mean by 'Christianity', then, is not the leavened lump of the Church, but the yeast that changes it (cf. Matthew 13.33). It is the salt (better, 'saltness') that goes into the stew and effects that miraculous shift from tasteless mishmash to something that is and will remain edible (cf. Matthew 5.13; Mark 9.49–50). To employ a more scientific metaphor, it is the catalyst that allows and empowers the chemical reaction. But the result of Christianity's action – its 'leavening', 'salting' or 'catalysis' – is a result. If you ask for yeast or salt at the corner shop, you will not be given bread or stew but something that in itself is hardly fit to be eaten at all, something that is only valued for its power to change something else.

When people use yeast to make bread, the yeast is used up in the process, because it is killed when the risen dough is heated in the oven. So it is no use mixing risen baked bread with new dough and expecting the transformation to continue. You need yeast to cause the change; that which it has changed retains no power of itself to change other things. In the same way, the newly prepared stockpot will need a new sprinkling of salt to give it taste; you won't get very far by putting in a pinch of already-salted soup. And in chemistry, although the catalyst is not destroyed by the chemical change that it facilitates, and can therefore be used to create another reaction, it is the catalyst that effects this second change, not the results of the catalyst's first reaction.

All metaphors break down eventually, and these may have broken down some time ago. More plainly: *The gospel cannot be passed on by passing on the Church.* Certainly, you cannot guarantee to pass on the gospel ('that which is the saltness of the salt') by replicating any present Christian community, its thoughts and its ways. Even if that community has responded obediently to the gospel, it remains only a response – and, inevitably, a particular response. It is *their* response. The case is even stronger if we focus, as we must, on individuals. It may be that by successfully transmitting your beliefs, values and behaviour to me, you will ensure that I too shall discern the true gospel and respond to it in my turn. But my response will be a new reaction, not a continuation or replication of your old one. I will have found the gospel through you, rather than in you. Hearing and seeing your response to the gospel I will have heard and seen the gospel for myself, and reacted to it for myself.

Thus Christianity is always a new beginning, and that beginning is a particular thing. Each one is different. Learning Christ is consequently always a new learning. To believe Christianity at all, to respond to it at all, to follow it at all, to do it at all, I must and can only do it 'my way'.

On the way

Now where have we heard that before? Despite its rather odd lyrics, and the apparent references to death in the first verse, Frank Sinatra's signature song remains a favourite for many – even for requests on hospital radio! I suppose it captures something of the defiant spirit of personal choice and decision that characterizes our age. At least, and without regrets, 'I did it my way.'

Inevitably, the philosophers were there first. Friedrich Nietzsche put these words into the mouth of Zarathustra (the founder of the ancient Zoroastrian faith): ' "This – is now *my* way: where is yours?" Thus I answered those who asked me "the way". For *the* way – does not exist!' Christians may want to express it rather differently. But, surely, there is no other way that the Way can become the Way for me, without it being followed and learned in my way? Therefore no minister or priest or congregation or denomination is of any use to me unless they can help me in that; unless they will walk with me on my road. Along that journey they will share their own vision and wisdom, and their distinctive and unique friendship, but if they are realistic (and if they care about me) they will do it all for only one purpose – to help me walk my way. Thus do we learn Christ, each in our routine, ordinary way. And only thus can we learn Christ *together*.

I may seem to be labouring a very simple point here. Unfortunately, it is a principle that I have taken rather a long time to grasp, because it has taken me that long to twig that I do after all know myself better than anyone else does. I've got the hang of me now. I know what works for me; I know what I need and want. I now know when my prejudices, my 'prejudgements', are just narrow and ignorant hasty assessments; and I know when they have been tested and proved and will not be – and should not be – budged. And I know what can save me.

These are the deep truths that I know about myself, and about what can make me whole. They are my salvific truths. You will have your own truths of this kind. We had better stick with what we know; for I believe that this is God's particular, personal revelation to us. It is also God's particular salvation for us, and the unique word of Christ to us.

Obviously we shall learn from others (more than before, perhaps, when we admit what we already know ourselves). We shall learn from the past. We are each called to paint our own portrait of Christianity; yet, like most artists, this act of personal creativity will be informed, enhanced and enlivened by viewing the work of other painters. Original artists are helped, not hindered, by visiting art galleries.

Despite my plea for individuality in Chapter 3, there is no excuse for rampant spiritual isolationism. Christians today should continue to learn from the tradition and revelation of the past. But that learning must be for a purpose that is neither antiquarian nor voyeuristic (nor 'merely' academic). In the words of the psychologist James Day, Christian faith is 'something we're invited into, not as a museum but as a living conversation.' And, as with the tango, it takes two to talk.

The past talks, but so must we.

A new beginning?

Christianity in the third millennium will eventually be, for the whole Church, the same as before – and yet totally different. It will be in its pure form the same faith, the same demand and the same gospel. But its expression must now be more internally varied and multi-dimensional, more personal and experiential, more lay and more humble. Pray God, the Christian Church will thus become more *human*. It will have to accept its own variety, and acknowledge its plural humanity. Only in this way can it come closer to Christ.

To enable this, much of the old must die to us. If we are honest, much of it has already died. Accepting that death may yet allow a resurrection of a new Church, but only if we believe in the necessity of death as much as we hope for the possibility of resurrection. In each age, as in each person, Christianity must begin all over again.

Our ordinary Christian life should share these qualities, by being more humble and more human. These are today the only ways in which we can come closer to Christ, and reveal and express him – becoming as little Christs in our own age and on our own roads.

Perhaps that is something that is even more significant than resurrection. It might be what the Church has yearned for, over two thousand years. The *parousia*.

This is the New Testament's word for the 'second coming' of Christ. It derives from a verb that means 'to be beside' or 'to be present'. About Christ's second coming, no one knows, not even him (Mark 13.32). Nevertheless, if we know ourselves, we should know a little of the possibility, the means and the extent of our everyday pilgrimage in the way of Christ, across our vastly varied lives. We should already know, then, something about where, when and how Christ is formed there. Dare we say that to know this is already to know something of his *parousia* – his presence, his arrival – in us?

To learn Christ on the road, to become his disciple in our ordinary way, is to become as him. Here.

That is the new beginning. It is the new presence of Jesus, on the road, in us. And that beginning must also be The End, for it is the point and the purpose of life. It represents the deepest depth of the Christian story. There may be much more to come, but this is as far as we need to see.

It will not be easy, though, this coming into labour, bearing through the loss and death of the old Church and the old ways to allow the rebirth of the new life of Christ, in and through ourselves. Birth and death are rarely easy. And uncovering depth is always hard labour.

8

The multifaceted Jesus

> Jesus went on with his disciples to the villages of Caesarea Philippi; and on the way he asked his disciples, 'Who do people say that I am?' And they answered him . . .
>
> He asked them, 'But who do you say that I am?'
>
> *Mark 8.27–29*

At last we return to the beginning. This happens on their road, this interrogation about the meaning of Jesus. He wants to know what other people make of him, how they view him. But he particularly wants to know what the disciples think. They are following him, but what – and how – do they see? Has his vision 'taken' with them? 'How do *you* see me?'

Try to forget that joke about the self-opinionated man (no, it's not a tautology) out on the first date telling the woman about himself at length and concluding, 'That's enough about me. Now tell me what you think about me.' Or if you can't forget it, reflect that this might be the fundamental – though usually unvoiced – question that arises in and challenges every relationship.

I suppose it all depends who's asking.

What have we learned – on our everyday roads – of this Jesus, this Christ? For us, as for the first disciples, this is a question not only about the object of our vision and learning but also about ourselves. What is it for me to learn *Christ*? Who do I say that he is?

Viewing Jesus

To start with I want to argue that learning Christ must begin with looking on Jesus *as* the Christ. This is a matter of seeing Jesus in that particular way, as 'God's anointed', God's representative, God's man. 'Christ' is not, of course, another name; it is not Jesus' surname. It is a title: 'Jesus, the Christ'. To speak of Christ at all, therefore, is to view the historical figure of Jesus as Lord. And this too is a human vision or perspective; if we are Christians, it is our vision or perspective. Inevitably the 'Christ of faith' is, at least in part, the Christ of our faith. As Christ is always Christ-for-us, our reading of Christ is always going to be our reading of what is important to us and what has significance for us. And that will be dependent on what we find in the figure of the historical Jesus that evokes our respect – and our worship. 'All those can be called Christian,' wrote Hans Küng, 'for whom in life and death Jesus Christ is ultimately decisive.'

'The Christ of our faith.' As the last chapter noted, there are a lot of us about and we are a very varied lot. So we must concede that there are going to be many different perspectives on Jesus. Patently, that has always been the case (although this variety has often been suppressed by the Church). It has been said that there is *one* Jesus but *many* Christs.

> I call him Christ insofar as I respond to this summons [to acknowledge the reality of God] and find in the gospels the pattern or shape of what it is to obey it. But the way he is Christ for me may be very different from the way he is Christ for some other person.

So wrote Don Cupitt, at a less radical stage of his theological career.

Since we can worship only that to which we ascribe supreme worth, our reading of Christ will uncover what *we* really value – our sense, if you like (and if you like the language of orthodoxy), of what it is to be fully human and what it is to be fully divine. Only a Christ who embodies these attributes need reply to the job advert we have framed.

I was once involved in some research that discovered a 'positive correlation' between people's individual psychology and the image they held of Jesus. In other words, we found that extraverts tend to image Jesus as sociable, lively and talkative; whereas introverts are more likely to see him as a quiet person who kept in the background. The tender-minded were inclined to think of Jesus as having a rather unselfish, warm personality; while tough-minded folk leaned towards a harder and more impersonal image of Jesus.

Should we be scandalized by this? I don't think so. Isn't it inescapable? It is simply an aspect of the claim that Christ is the one for us.

Reflecting on reflections

At the beginning of the last century, the Protestant Adolf Harnack published a book in which he portrayed a Jesus who was very different from the one traditionally proclaimed by the Church. The problem, as the English scholar–priest George Tyrrell graphically put it, was that what Harnack saw, as he peered back through 19 dark centuries, was 'the reflection of a Liberal Protestant face, seen at the bottom of a deep well'. Looking for Jesus, Harnack had found only himself, and therefore described Jesus as a nineteenth-century liberal preacher of Protestant morality and rational piety. 'Whatever Jesus was,' Tyrrell wrote, 'He was in no sense a Liberal Protestant.'

Hard words indeed, even for academics in dispute (which they mostly are). Should we care? It is natural to hope that we can get back behind the overlaying levels of later doctrinal interpretations to the real Jesus of history. How far New Testament scholars can succeed in this task is much disputed. Whether they do so or not, we should note that what the scholars are seeking is Jesus, the 'Jesus of history'. Our concern in this chapter, however, is much more clearly and explicitly with the Christ of faith. This is *our Jesus*. The Christ for us is the Jesus who speaks to us and who speaks for us; inevitably, he is the one to whom our ears are already attuned. This is almost a tautology: the Jesus we notice is the one who is noticeable to us. He is our Lord, our Christ, our Saviour.

On this interpretation, there can never be a truly objective, neutral account of *Christ*, even if one were possible of the historical Jesus. 'Simply because he is admired and believed in . . . we cannot help intruding ourselves into the picture we form and see', as one writer has put it. If shaping Jesus in one's own image is an ever-present element in scholarship, so that Albert Schweitzer can say that 'there is no historical task which so reveals a man's true self as the writing of a Life of Jesus', how much more will the disciple's image of Christ reveal her own concerns?

If we cannot help it, then Tyrrell's stricture is too harsh. We need to amend his picture not only to soften the language, but also to counter its implication of an uncontrolled relativism. Leaning over the rim of the well of Christian history, doctrine and piety, our view of Christ – our 'Christology', to use the technical term – is not merely a self-serving, wholly subjective invention; nothing more than wishful thinking. There is something down there to be seen.

The metaphor contains the clue to its own reformulation. Reflections in water are never just pure self-reflections, provided that the water that generates them is sufficiently shallow. For in that case, when looking down a well or into a pool we shall often see a virtual image of our own faces overlaying a real – though distorted, muddied and shifting – glimpse of whatever it is that lies below the water. As in Chapter 6, the figure of speech we are concerned with here involves a confluence of images, and the effects which that can evoke. And, as before, we must think of one of those images as belonging to Jesus. Imagine, then, looking down a well whose bottom is covered by a mosaic picture of the face of Jesus. Under the right conditions – with a lot of light and not much water – we would see the image of Jesus and that of our own face somehow superimposed, even blended. Reflection and refraction would go together.

The same situation obtains in reading any significant text, or in any deep interpersonal relationship. So it is sometimes said that in reading the Bible, Christians are also 'reading themselves'; and in knowing you I also come to know myself. What is true of human friendship is true of other perceptions, visions and relationships: 'If I were pressed to say why I love him, I feel that my only reply could be: "Because it was he, because it was I" ' (see p. 49).

This is particularly significant in the case of seeking, seeing, finding and embracing one's Lord. While it is still possible for Jesus to be 'the critic rather than the mere endorser' of the beliefs of his disciples (see p. 102), we must honestly recognize that 'learning Christ' is no neutral scientific or historical exercise in which it doesn't matter who *we* are at all. The claim that Jesus is my Lord says something about me as well as a great deal about him.

We claim Jesus for ourselves, or we reject him for ourselves. Tender-minded introvert that I am (or macho extravert that I am not), he is *my* Lord and my Saviour. I value him, celebrate him, worship him; I find my peace and wholeness and healing in him. He is 'salvific' for me. As the word isn't in the standard dictionaries, I should have defined it before. Theologians employ it because they need a word for *that which brings us salvation*. The salvific is whatever keeps us safe from – and if needs be rescues us from – harm, ruin or loss. More positively, it is whatever heals us and makes us whole again.

Here is one important sense in which Christ is always *for us*, a sense in which we have some stake in the meaning and message of Christ. Jesus would not have been Christ without the disciples: without people who recognized him as such. More broadly, the Kingdom of God only works – it only becomes real – when people see it and hear it, acknowledge and embrace it. Without this vision both the people and (from one point of view) their Lord perish.

I should have said 'without these visions'. The Church includes the great variegated, multiple, rich variety of all these different perspectives on Jesus, who is not only my Lord and yours (if he is) but the Lord of all of us, the 'Lord of the Church'. It is no accident that so many different disciples were and are eventually called together on to one road. The Church can and must create a profound and expressive harmony of praise from this variety of visions and this variety of voices (as we individually find our own voice to express our own vision – to change the imagery). In this anthem of the one Church we each have our own part to sing. And no one can sing it for us.

How did I put it in the last chapter? 'There is no other way that the Way can become the Way for me, without it being followed and learned in my way.' 'Thus do we learn Christ, each in our routine, ordinary way.' And in Christ, all these different pathways run together along the one broad-yet-narrow highway that constitutes the way of true living. This is one interpretation of Jesus' prayer that these many may all be one (John 17).

But first we must be ourselves and let others be themselves, in Christ and for his sake.

The many sides of Jesus

'One Jesus, many Christs.' Some Christians seem hung up on getting the one right interpretation of everything that is even remotely Christian, so that the line between orthodoxy and heresy becomes clearly marked and effectively patrolled. To what end, I wonder? This is the instinct of people with something to lose – power, perhaps, or control. Status?

It is hardly the way of Jesus, or even of Paul. Jesus seems to have allowed people to answer the question, 'Who do you say that I am', in their own, very disparate ways. Even when Peter answered, 'You are the Messiah', Jesus 'sternly ordered them not to tell anyone about him' (Mark 8.30). At first sight, Paul comes over as a very different character, and much more likely to insist on right opinions and correct responses. Nevertheless, the maxim he adopts for his own behaviour could have come from the lips of Jesus himself:

For though I am free with respect to all, I have made myself a slave to all, so that I might win more of them. To the Jews I became as a Jew, in order to win Jews . . . To those outside the law I became

117

as one outside the law . . . so that I might win those outside the law. To the weak I became weak, so that I might win the weak. I have become all things to all people, so that I might by any means save some. I do it all for the sake of the gospel . . .

(1 Corinthians 9.19–23)

It is not that Paul was not a certain sort of person, someone who was like this rather than that. And there is no doubt that the mind, words and works of Jesus also had a specific, determinate character. But these central figures of our faith are big enough to have many different sides, from which we different people may select and emphasize different aspects. In the case of Jesus, particularly, there is 'something for everyone'; and that something is enough for each of us.

Welcome, then, to the multidimensional Jesus. Why should we want him to be anything else?

So when I read the Gospels, searching among the words of Jesus and the words about Jesus for my saviour, the main reason that I turn up a different Christ from yours – if I do – is not that we disagree about any historical facts, believing that he says or does different things (although we might do, as academics often do). The crucial factor is that certain of Jesus' actions and words have a significance for me that they do not have for you. We cannot ignore this difference if our religious reflections are to be honest – as they must be. I insist again that we should speak first (if not only) of what we *know*, and stop pretending to agree where we do not agree. Especially, we should not pretend that we find healing in locations where we have not ourselves been healed.

The salvation brought by Jesus to the woman who had suffered haemorrhages for 12 years (Mark 5.24b–34) was very different from the salvation brought to the rich tax collector Zacchaeus (Luke 19.1–10). This was because their needs were different, their hurts different and their sins different. And if *I* am to say, 'You are the Christ, the Son of the Blessed', it can only be because *my* needs have been met, my hurts healed, and my sinfulness and misunderstandings challenged, redeemed and resolved.

The woman would not have been wrong to say 'he is a healer', nor would Zacchaeus have been wrong to say 'he welcomes sinners'. Nor, in the familiar legend, were any of the blind men standing around the elephant wrong to say that what they touched with their hands was likely a serpent, a fan or a banana plant. Each one spoke truly on the basis of his limited experience. All knowledge of another, even of the one Jesus, is partial and particular. But this is not my main point, for in religion we have to do with a particular type of knowledge – with saving knowledge, which is knowledge that forms part of a particular species of *relationship*. This ratchets up the situation several notches. All our relationships with one another are partly determined by the several natures, needs and interests of the different people involved. But our healing relationship with this one Jesus is subject to this qualification in an even more extreme form. It is different for me from the way it is for you not simply because we are not one and the same person, but because we therefore need saving from and for different things – and in different ways.

Here again we uncover a proper and wholly acceptable, even inevitable, form of relativism: 'salvific relativism'. This partly explains, I think, the way in which any account of Christ seems to lose its religious power, value and therefore (in one sense, at least) its *truth*, the further it departs from the particular saving perspective that first evoked it. Attempts by the Church or academic theology to convey a 'more complete' and systematic Christology leave most people cold.

Can you stomach another metaphor? Pearls are formed of concentric layers of nacre ('mother of pearl'), the perfectly spherical specimens being the ones that are most highly valued. As these would be spoiled by cutting, we do not have many-sided pearls – at any rate not 'of great value' (Matthew 13.46). Diamonds are different. Usually more precious than pearls, their beauty is further enhanced by suitable cutting. In the case of these particular precious stones, the more and better the cuts made to them, the more we value them. Jesus may be likened to such a diamond. He is the multifaceted jewel of the Christian treasury.

This time it's personal

Let me say how all this works for me. How do I view Jesus; how do I read Christ?

I perform my viewing and reading in a rather one-sided, partial and partisan way. I do it my way, as you do. However, I hope that my view and reading are consistent with many of the stories about Jesus presented in the Gospels, and can give some coherence to the rather disparate set of traditions about Jesus that we find there. I imagine that few will deny that the elements I point to are present in these Jesus traditions, although others may resist to varying degrees the significance and interpretation I give to the passages below.

Looking at the Gospels with the sort of eye I have, derived from the sort of beliefs I have, the main features of my portrait of Jesus the Christ stand out clearly. Many of my concerns relate to questions about a person's perceived value, importance, position, esteem, 'standing' – in a word, his or her outer *status*. 'Central to traditional Christian thought,' writes Alain de Botton, 'was the claim that one's status carried no moral connotations.' Social superiority is not moral superiority. Remember, 'Jesus did not look on the face of men' (Chapter 2).

My reading of the New Testament finds a man who was born with little status, who called a motley band of no-ones-in-particular, and who taught and lived a Kingdom that was 'not of this world' partly because it demanded the self-denial of status – and especially of any moral and religious status. He died in ignominy, without any status: covered with the grime of the world, hard by the rubbish tips.

This is the Christ of humility, who takes our breath away with his radical overturning of our concerns and assumptions about our own hard-won standing and dignity, before God and in the face of our colleagues, neighbours, strangers – and even our lovers, families and friends.

Jesus' resurrection was not a reversal of any of this, as if the giving up of status is only an interim ethic along the road to the attainment of a greater status. This cannot be the case, for the resurrection itself, as we saw in Chapter 7, was without status. Even now, it is known only by those who are able to see power in weakness, stature in humility and victory on a cross. The resurrection wasn't a slap in the face for those who reviled the crucified Jesus, shouting, 'Save yourself and come down.' The risen Christ did not come back like the United States Cavalry, publicly wielding a new power and position so as to teach his doubters a lesson. All talk of that sort of thing is deferred to another age, the mysterious 'apocalyptic' future (as in Mark 13.26 and 14.62). At Easter he returned secretly. The resurrection has already come to the cowed, the broken and the hopeless; it seems to have been reserved for those who 'need to know'.

Jesus' resurrection is thus of a piece with his life and his death, which was, we recall, the life and death of one who 'emptied himself, taking the form of a slave ... humbled himself and became obedient to the point of death – even death on a cross' (Philippians 2.7–8).

'Lord, is this the time when you will restore the kingdom to Israel?', the apostles ask, uncomprehending to the end (Acts 1.6). The answer is, more or less, 'Of course not. Please don't be so stupid.' The only power he will give them from on high is the power to be witnesses – that is, martyrs – and makers of disciples; and the power to hold all things in common and to distribute their goods to those in need.

That is how I see him, as an 'everyday', 'commonplace' Christ. But what is the evidence for this reading?

I can list some of it. There are the words of the Magnificat, which celebrate God's choice of lowliness and his scattering of the proud: 'He has brought down the powerful from their thrones, and lifted up the lowly' (Luke 1.52). This text is followed closely by Luke's narrative of Jesus' humbling birth, which the low-status shepherds are called to attend. Later, there is the denial of signs and power in the temptations; the ministry to and table fellowship with the religious outcasts; the Beatitudes, in which the poor, the meek and the persecuted are pronounced blessed; the words spoken against the rich and those who seek religious status; and the high role given to low-status women among Jesus' followers, even so far as their serving as witnesses to the resurrection. Then there is the teaching about the greatness of those who serve and about the servant role Jesus himself takes – as the one who washes his disciples' feet, and the 'Son of Man' who has no place to lay his head. There is the praise of the widow's mite, and the acted parable in which the low-status child is presented as the model of true discipleship and the key to entering God's Kingdom. There is also the persuasive definition of where true treasure lies; and the self-deprecating language that Jesus uses of himself – 'Why do you call me good?' (Mark 10.18), 'Who set me to be a judge or arbitrator over you?' (Luke 12.14).

I could appeal to other features of the sort of figure that Jesus cut among his contemporaries: as one who does not himself esteem position, and who is symbolized – but remains unrecognized – in the 'least ones', the 'little ones' (Chapter 6). We might also note the enjoining of poverty in the disciples' early missionary work; the parable of the Pharisee and tax collector; Jesus' entry into Jerusalem on a young, common and lowly ass; the silence and humiliation of his trial; and the curse of the cross itself.

Interwoven with all these acts, words and silences is the central theme of the Kingdom of God, 'God's reign', which involves a radical reversal of status. In that Kingdom the first shall be last, 'for all who exalt themselves will be humbled, but all who humble themselves will be exalted' (Luke 14.11; 18.14; Matthew 23.12). First and foremost this is a gospel for the *poor*, in the widest sense – good news for the helpless and oppressed, including those who live out their lives on the social and religious margins (Luke 4.18).

Naturally, the rich, healthy and successful don't reckon it, particularly those who are religiously successful. 'Beware of practising your piety before others in order to be seen by them . . . as the hypocrites do . . . so that they may be praised by others. Truly I tell you, they have received their reward' (Matthew 6.1–2). What reward is that, then? Presumably it is the reward of the admiration that bestows success, and specifically bestows status. If you want to be admired for your piety then you know how to achieve that end, Jesus seems to say. The rewards for such behaviour are self-evident and guaranteed. If that is what you want, then that is what you will get. Hence 'those who are well', especially those who enjoy a healthy moral and religious status, will feel no need of the healing good news of God's acceptance. Jesus, however, is physician to the sick (Mark 2.17). 'The poor' of the Psalms and Beatitudes, and 'the humble' of the Magnificat – those who are of low status, they are 'no people'. Yet the gospel is given to them; their poverty starkly underscoring the fact that they could neither afford nor demand it. 'Do not be afraid, little flock, for it is your Father's good pleasure to give you the kingdom' (Luke 12.32).

Many of these passages express the claim that Jesus' status-denying stance and ministry are to be shared by his disciples also. The disciple–learner is not above his master in this way either (Matthew 10.24–25; John 15.20). They have a very clear guide as to how to learn Christ, 'for I am gentle and humble in heart . . . my yoke is easy, and my burden is light' (Matthew 11.29–30).

> I have set you an example, that you also should do as I have done to you. Very truly, I tell you, servants are not greater than their master; nor are messengers greater than the one who sent them. If you know these things, you are blessed if you do them.
>
> (John 13.15–17)

At one level, then, these are the 'sources' for my Christology. I claim that Jesus is like this in the New Testament. If we have any evidence for Jesus, we have evidence of his views about status, and his actions in transcending its divisions and rankings. Others read the Gospels differently. They emphasize different features, and may therefore find a rather different Jesus from mine. I cannot believe, however, that he could be wholly different from this.

But I don't pretend to be a New Testament scholar. Luckily, many real scholars give a similar account. Here is Joel Green, for example, writing with reference to the context of Roman culture.

On the one hand, we find evidence in the gospel narratives of 'business as usual' among Jesus' followers, as they vie for places of honour. Who is the greatest? Jesus' response to this sort of posturing for social position was to place before his disciples a little child ... Serve these most vulnerable persons, these of lowest status, with honour; the dominion of God belongs to such persons. Here is a far-reaching inversion of Roman ideology. On the other, in the context of a world carefully managed by a system of reciprocity and patronage, Jesus insisted that people give without expectation of return. The household of Rome was built on social norms in which the giving of gifts (whether goods and services or invitations to banquets) brought with it expectations of reciprocity. Here was a systematic segregation of those of relative status from the dispossessed, since the latter were incapable either of advancing the social status of the former or even of returning the favour of an invitation to hospitality. Jesus set forth for his audiences an alternative household not characterised by concerns with debt and obligation. Services were to be performed and gifts given to others as though they were family, 'without expectation of return' ...

Deep-rooted dispositions towards acquiring, claiming and maintaining relative status and power surface throughout the gospel tradition, and Jesus consistently censures them – for example, when he gives advice on dinner invitations and seating arrangements (Luke 14.1–24) and when he urges hospitality to the least impressive inhabitants of the Roman social world, little children ... Jesus ... profoundly subverts status-seeking practices by directing his disciples to comport themselves as slaves rather than despotic rulers.

But hang on a minute. This discussion is not just about the historical *Jesus*. Didn't I claim that we were looking for a *Christ*, a *Saviour*? Even when the best biblical scholars have had their say, the rest of us still have to decide whether the pictures they paint of Jesus will do *for us*. Can their Jesus – this Jesus – be our Christ?

In my search for a Christ I will view the biblical texts in a particular way, interrogating them from, with and through a set of deeply held values. I shall seek in the Scriptures what is relevant, significant and important to me. And I shall hope to find there an account that is salvific for me. There may be more to Jesus than this, but I shall have to declare that this is what saves me. So anything that reduces the significance of the elements in the Gospels that are most salient for me would in the end be of no use to me.

The values I hold – the moral and spiritual values that serve as focusing lenses for my identification of Christ – are the values that motivate this overturning of the world's distinctions of status. I hold them very close; and I hold them to be Christ-ian values. They explain a lot about me. They explain my feelings about those within the Church who seem to lust after the demonic aphrodisiac of 'becoming someone' in the eyes of themselves and the world – and thus implicitly (but completely) reversing the plain direction of Jesus' teaching, by loading the notion of a person's status with moral connotations. When you know the things you are for, you also know what you are against.

Very personal

As yet, however, I have told you nothing about *why* I see things like this. Where did this insistence on the overturning of status come from? How did these values become my values?

Evidently I did not just read them off the pages of the Bible. Rather, I am encouraged to find and emphasize them there because I already care for them. These are the values I yearn for, so they make this scripture holy to me. We all do something like this. Christians don't get their Christianity solely from the New Testament; not even biblical fundamentalists do that. Much of what is key to us in our faith is already part of our way of seeing things. It constitutes the lenses of the spectacles that bring our reading of our sacred texts into sharp focus. I see Jesus the Christ like this, and I see everything like this, because of something about me.

Whence, then, came my values? That is a difficult question for anyone to answer. It may also prove to be an embarrassing one.

Did I think them up for myself? Well, they do now seem natural to me. So maybe they are partly a consequence of my particular, and perhaps peculiar, psychology. But I believe that the greater part of our values are *learned*. We now own them; but we learned them from other people, mostly informally and often unconsciously, as they seeped through the gaps and chinks of our daily lives, experiences and relationships (Chapters 1 and 7).

To be frank, most of mine came from my mother.

She had no status. At least, no one ever thought of her as having any sort of superior status, and she never thought of herself in that way either. She wasn't 'someone'. She was 'just ordinary', as if that were not enough. A defining moment in my view of her, and in the development of my take on the Christian gospel, happened at some church jamboree. Despite being a life-long Anglican churchgoer, she visibly shrank because she felt too small and insignificant to shake the hand of some ecclesiastic who was passing by, dripping condescension. Unfortunately, I was sufficiently familiar with him to know a truth that neither of them would ever have believed: that he was wholly unworthy to untie my mother's shoe.

To my great shame, I never really knew her as well as she deserved to be known. But throughout her hard life of self-giving she certainly expressed for me what it was to be Christian. She was flawed, as everyone is; but I am happy to apply to her – with the pronouns appropriately modified – the words that one famous, high-status Christian once applied to another (Austin Farrer, speaking of C. S. Lewis). 'She really was a Christian – by which I mean, she never thought she had the right to stop.'

For me, that's where it comes from. No other Christ will do for me because of that, because of her. That life and that example is where, and how, I learned Christ.

I wonder if something like that may not be true for you as well. I don't know whether it is, because I don't know you; and I never knew your mother either. Only *you* know how you learned Christ, why and how it is that you are a Christian, if you are. Only you know the foundations of your everyday faith.

Of the many dimensions of Jesus, this is the one that saves me – the facet marked by these particular values and this particular gospel. And I have lately come to realize that it is the only one that can save me. By contrast, any Jesus who made his apologies and left as he was about to sit down to a meal with the sinners, or was on the point of healing the blind, and who took off solely because he had received a better invitation from the better-connected – such a Jesus could not be Christ to me. And now we both know why.

To know who is the Christ of your everyday – and why he is that – is to know yourself, in him. It is to have learned Christ in your way.

That is the beginning – and it is the end – of the wisdom of the road.

Acknowledgements, references and further reading

Much of this material originated in a course of talks for Lent given at Durham Cathedral. I am grateful to Margaret Parker for her invitation, and to the audiences in Prior's Hall for their comments and questions, some of which I have responded to in the text. Part of Chapter 2 was also first given as a sermon in Durham Cathedral; I am grateful to Alex Whitehead for his invitation. Chapter 8 began life as an open lecture at Durham University and has been on various outings since, most recently at a study day for the Diocese of Blackburn. Again my thanks go to those who invited me to speak and to those who listened, questioned and argued on these occasions.

I have reworked all this material and I am very grateful to Evelyn Jackson for patiently typing and retyping the manuscript.

I note below details of the passages I quote in the text, together with some suggestions for further reading. My thanks are due to the publishers who have granted permission to quote from works under copyright, beyond the limits of 'fair dealing'. Unless otherwise indicated, quotations from the Bible are from the New Revised Standard Version Bible, copyright © 1989 by the Division of Christian Education of the National Council of the Churches of Christ in the USA, and are used by permission. All rights reserved.

1 On learning Christ in the ordinary way

The first quotation is from Don Cupitt, *Life, Life*. Polebridge Press, Santa Rosa, Calif., 2003, p. 50; the quotation ends 'and petty celebrity worship', on which topic see the next chapter. The 'writer on preaching' is Fred Craddock: see David Day, Jeff Astley and Leslie J. Francis (eds), *A Reader on Preaching: Making Connections*. Ashgate, Aldershot, 2005, p. 92 (the biblical reference is to John 19.26–27). Wittgenstein's comment on philosophy is in his *Philosophical Investigations*. Blackwell, Oxford, 1967, part I, paragraph 124. William Blake's aphorism is from a letter collected in G. Keynes (ed.), *Poetry and Prose of William Blake*. Nonesuch, London, 1961, p. 835, part of a passage in praise of the imagination. For Blake (a painter as well as a poet), this world is 'a world of Imagination and Vision'. The quotations that follow are from Søren Kierkegaard, *Edifying Discourses: A Selection*, edited by Paul L. Holmer, Collins, London, 1958, p. 68, and Karl Barth, *Church Dogmatics*, Vol. IV/1. Edinburgh, T. & T. Clark, 1956, p. 725. In my account of discipleship I quote Leslie Houlden, *Paul's Letters from Prison: Philippians, Colossians, Philemon and Ephesians*. Penguin, Harmondsworth, 1970, p. 318; K. H. Rengstorf's article on *mathetes* in Gerhard Kittel (ed.), *Theological Dictionary of the New Testament*, Vol. IV. Eerdmans, Grand Rapids, Mich., 1967, p. 449; Charles F. Melchert, *Wise Teaching: Biblical Wisdom and Educational Ministry*. Trinity Press International, Harrisburg, Penn., 1998, p. 224; and T. W. Manson, *The Teaching of Jesus: Studies of Its Form and Content*. Cambridge University Press, Cambridge, 1935, pp. 238–9. The final quotations are from Craig Dykstra, *Growing in the Life of Faith: Education and Christian Practices*. Geneva Press, Louisville, Ky., 1999, p. 160, and Graham Chapman, et al., *Monty Python's Flying Circus*, Vol. 2. London, Methuen, 1989, pp. 93–4.

Other things to read

Others who treat the theology and spirituality of the ordinary include John Drury, *Angels and Dirt: An Enquiry into Theology and Prayer*. Darton, Longman & Todd, London, 1972; Michael Frost, *Seeing God in the Ordinary: A Theology of the Everyday*. Hendrickson, Peabody, Mass., 2000; and Paul L. Holmer, *The Grammar of Faith*. Harper & Row, San Francisco, Calif., 1978. Three more radical books are Don Cupitt's *The New Religion of Life in Everyday Speech* (1999), *The Meaning of It All in Everyday Speech* (1999) and *Kingdom Come in Everyday Speech* (2000) (all SCM, London). A much lighter approach may be found in Jeff Astley and David Day (eds), *Beyond the Here and Now*. Lion, Oxford, 1996. I have written an apologia for non-academic religious reflection in *Ordinary Theology: Looking, Listening and Learning in Theology*. Ashgate, Aldershot, 2002.

2 The deeper gospel

The first quotation on fame is from Howard Sounes, *Down the Highway: The Life of Bob Dylan*. Grove Press, New York, 2001, p. 270. The American artist Andy Warhol commented that 'in the future, everyone will be world famous for fifteen minutes' in a catalogue of an exhibition of his art, Stockholm, 1968. Oliver James' views are in *Britain on the Couch: Why We're Unhappier Compared with 1950 Despite Being Richer*. Random House, London, 1998, pp. 110 and 333. Alain de Botton's comments are from his excellent study, *Status Anxiety*. Hamish Hamilton, London, 2004, pp. 3–4 and 260 (see also p. 157). Kipling's 'When Earth's Last Picture is Painted' (1892) is in T. S. Eliot (ed.), *A Choice of Kipling's Verse*. Faber & Faber, London, 1963, p. 110. Pages 4, 8 and 76 from the English translation of Martin Buber's *Ich und Du* ('*I and Thou*') (T. & T. Clark, Edinburgh, 1959) are quoted on p. 21. The dialogue between Granny Weatherwax and the priest is in Terry Pratchett, *Carpe Jugulum*. Corgi, London, 1999, pp. 313–14. The church leaver is cited in Philip Richter and Leslie J. Francis, *Gone But Not Forgotten: Church Leaving and Returning*. Darton, Longman & Todd, London, 1998, p. 106. The 'thick' disciple – then and now – is described by William C. Spohn, *Go and Do Likewise: Jesus and Ethics*. Continuum, New York, 1999, pp. 31, 101.

Other things to read

Terry Pratchett's witty and imaginative fantasy novels contain much 'moral shrewdness' (as A. S. Byatt has put it) and depth (as I would put it), in an irreverent and iconoclastic form – see especially *Mort* (Corgi, London, 1988) and *Small Gods* (Corgi, London, 1993). On divine mystery, see Andrew Louth, *Discerning the Mystery*. Oxford University Press, Oxford, 1983. On interpersonal (and intrapersonal) intelligence, see Howard Gardner, *Frames of Mind: The Theory of Multiple Intelligences*. HarperCollins, London, 1993, chapter 10; on emotional intelligence, see Daniel Goleman, *Emotional Intelligence*. Bantam Books, New York, 1995. For a rather secular account of spiritual intelligence, see Danah Zohar and Ian Marshall, *Spiritual Intelligence: The Ultimate Intelligence*. Bloomsbury, London, 2000.

3 In and out of the desert

The verses by Robert Frost are from his poem 'Desert Places' (1936), in Edward Connery Latham (ed.), *The Poetry of Robert Frost*. Jonathan Cape, London, 1971. Reproduced by permission of The Random House Group Ltd and Henry Holt and Company, LLC. Copyright 1975 by Lesley Frost Ballantine. A. N. Wilson's experience is recounted in *Jesus*. HarperCollins, London, 1993, p. 109. I quote from Rowan Williams' *The Wound of Knowledge*. Darton, Longman & Todd, London, 1979, pp. 95, 98, and his 'Desert, Desert Fathers', in Gordon S. Wakefield (ed.), *A Dictionary of Christian Spirituality*. SCM, London, 1983, p. 110. The quotation from Parker J. Palmer is from *To Know as We are Known: Education as a Spiritual Journey*. HarperSanFrancisco, San Francisco, Calif., 1993, p. 73; he writes perceptively on silence and solitude, 'in a wilderness where all things are mute', on pp. 117–24. Harry Williams' autobiography is entitled *Some Day I'll Find You*. Collins, London, 1984; I quote from pp. 193 and 354. His sermon on Lent is reprinted in *The True Wilderness*. Penguin, Harmondsworth, 1968 and Collins, London, 1979; I cite pp. 30, 33–4 of the earlier edition. 'Whatever else theology is . . .' comes from the preface to Williams' *True Resurrection*. Mitchell Beazley, London, 1972. The quotations from Thomas Merton and (later) Ammonas are from Kenneth Leech, *Soul Friend*. Sheldon, London, 1977, p. 140; I quote Leech's own words from pp. 141–2 later in the chapter. The Wordsworth quotation is from his *Miscellaneous Sonnets* (1, 33). The quote from John Wesley's Sermon 24 ('Upon Our Lord's Sermon on the Mount IV') is from his *Sermons on Several Occasions*. Epworth, London, 1944, p. 237. I also quote Alfred North Whitehead, *Religion in the Making*. Cambridge University Press, Cambridge, 1926, p. 16; Søren Kierkegaard, *Purity of Heart is to Will One Thing*. Harper & Row, New York, 1948, pp. 185, 191 and 193; and *Training in Christianity*. Princeton University Press, Princeton, N. J., 1941, p. 218. The quotation from C. S. Lewis' *The Horse and His Boy* (first published 1954) is from the Collins, London, 1980 edition, p. 139. Matthew Arnold's lines are from his 1852 poem, 'To Marguerite'; those from Thomas Hood (1799–1845) from his sonnet, 'Silence'. I quote Henri J. M. Nouwen, *The Way of the Heart: Desert Spirituality and Contemporary Ministry*. Darton, Longman & Todd, London, 1981, pp. 25–6; and Gareth Moore, *Believing in*

God: A Philosophical Essay. T. & T. Clark, Edinburgh, 1988, p. 190. The 'another' who writes against credulity and 'pixie-dust' is Don Cupitt, in *Only Human*. SCM, London, 1985, p. 200. I quote with the kind permission of Margo Ewart from Gavin Ewart's poem 'Prayer', first published in *The Listener*, 27 October 1977; it may be found in D. J. Enright (ed.), *The Oxford Book of Contemporary Verse 1945–1980*. Oxford University Press, Oxford, 1980, p. 78. The poems by R. S. Thomas, reproduced with kind permission, are in *The Echoes Return Slow*. Macmillan, London, 1988, p. 39 (© Kunjana Thomas 2001) and *Collected Poems 1945–1990*. J. M. Dent & Sons (a division of the Orion Publishers Group), London, 1993 ('Via Negativa' and 'The Absence'). I quote Carlo Carretto, *Letters from the Desert*. Darton, Longman & Todd, 1972, pp. 68–9, and John Donne's 'Hymn to Christ, at the Author's last going into Germany', from his *Poems* of 1633 (spelling slightly modernized).

Other things to read

John Habgood, *Varieties of Unbelief*. Darton, Longman & Todd, London, 2000, chapter 7; Richard Harries, *God Outside the Box: Why Spiritual People Object to Christianity*. SPCK, London, 2002, chapters 19 and 20; Andrew Louth, *The Wilderness of God*. Darton, Longman & Todd, London, 2003; Benedicta Ward, *The Desert Christian*. Macmillan, New York, 1975 and *The Wisdom of the Desert Fathers*. Lion, Oxford, 2002; Rowan Williams, *Silence and Honey Cakes: The Wisdom of the Desert*. Lion, Oxford, 2003. On prayer and acceptance, see Jean-Pierre de Caussade, SJ, *Self-Abandonment to Divine Providence*. Collins, Glasgow, 1971; Alan Ecclestone, *Yes to God*. Darton, Longman & Todd, London, 1975; and Henri J. M. Nouwen, *With Open Hands*. Ave Maria Press, Notre Dame, Ind., 1972, chapter 2. For more Harry Williams, see the anthology of his writings edited by Eileen Mable (*True to Experience*. Continuum, London, 2000).

4 With friends like these . . .

I have been unable to find a source for the quotation abbreviated in the title of this chapter. It is usually cited as an 'old saying' or 'aphorism', and sometimes as an 'old Jewish proverb'. Ralph Waldo

Emerson's reflections on 'Friendship' are from his *Essays* (1841); in 'The World's Classics' edition (Frowde, London, 1901), pp. 110–26. John Dryden's phrase is from his 'The Hind and the Panther' (1687), part III, lines 1341–2. The *Jewish Encyclopedia* entry is cited in W. M. Rankin, 'Friendship', in James Hastings (ed.), *Encyclopedia of Religion and Ethics*, Volume VI. T. & T. Clark, Edinburgh, 1913, p. 132. Stählin's article is in Volume IX of the *Theological Dictionary of the New Testament* (edited by Gerhard Friedrich) Eerdmans, Grand Rapids, Mich., 1974; I quote from pp. 156, 164. I refer to the scene 'Thursday night, The Last Supper' from *Jesus Christ Superstar* (1970) (libretto by Tim Rice). I quote Laura Marcus, 'All He Wants is the Sofa', *The Observer*. 17 September 2000, p. 31; C. S. Lewis, *The Four Loves*. Collins, London, 1963, p. 62; Donald Evans' excellent study on psychology, religion and morality, *Struggle and Fulfillment*. Collins, Cleveland, Ohio, 1979, pp. 129–39; De Montaigne's *Essays* in the translation by J. M. Cohen (Penguin, London, 1958), p. 97; and H. H. Price, Gifford Lectures, *Belief* (Allen & Unwin, London, 1969), pp. 453–4 (amended to make it more inclusive). Thomas Aquinas is cited from *Summa Contra Gentiles*, Book Four, chapter 22 (University of Notre Dame Press, Notre Dame, Ind., 1975, Volume 4, pp. 125–6). Aelred's twelfth-century text is called *Spiritual Friendship*; quotations are from Mark F. Williams' translation (Associated University Presses, London and Toronto, 1994, pp. 29, 41, 54). Robert Southwell (1561–95) is quoted from his poem, 'A Child My Choice', and Joseph Butler from his *Analogy of Religion* (1736), part II, chapter VI (p. 227 of W. E. Gladstone's edition, Clarendon, Oxford, 1896). The story about St Teresa is close to her reflection in the *Interior Castle* (mansion 6, chapter 11, paragraph 6): 'Alas, O Lord, to what a state dost Thou bring those who love Thee!' 'Open friendship' is discussed in Jürgen Moltmann, *The Spirit of Life: A Universal Affirmation*. Fortress Press, Minneapolis, Minn., 1992, pp. 255–9. The Walt Whitman quote is from 'I sing the Body Electric' (in *Walt Whitman: The Complete Poems*. Penguin, London, 1996, pp. 127–36); and Richard Hovey's from his play, *The Marriage of Guenevere: A Tragedy* (Act 1, Scene 1). Other quotations are from C. S. Lewis (ed.), *George MacDonald: An Anthology*. Collins, London, 1983, p. 124; Simone Weil's 'Spiritual Autobiography', from George A. Panichas (ed.), *The Simone Weil Reader*. David McKay, New York,

1977, p. 19; and Robert Grant's hymn, 'O worship the King all glorious above' (1833).

Other things to read

For Aristotle on friendship, see the *Nicomachean Ethics*, books 8 and 9. His account of friendship as the main aim of the moral life is summarized in Peter Vardy and Paul Grosch, *The Puzzle of Ethics*. HarperCollins, London, 1994, pp. 47–9. Alain de Botton traces the place of friendship for Epicurus and Montaigne in his accessible *The Consolations of Philosophy*. Penguin, London, 2001, pp. 56–8, 146–8. David Day and I have written briefly about friendship in *Beyond the Here and Now*. Lion, Oxford, 1996, chapter 40. I write about the particularity and universality of God's revelation and relationship in *God's World*. Darton, Longman & Todd, London, 2000, chapter 3. Jürgen Moltmann's *The Church in the Power of the Spirit*. SCM, London, 1977, describes the Church as 'the fellowship of friends who live in the friendship of Jesus' (p. 316); see also pp. 114–21 and 314–17. The strengths and weaknesses of the model of God as friend are discussed by Sallie McFague, *Metaphorical Theology: Models of God in Religious Language*. SCM, London, 1982, pp. 177–92. Other theological texts on friendship include Elisabeth Moltmann-Wendel, *Rediscovering Friendship*. SCM, London, 2000, and E. D. H. (Liz) Carmichael, *Friendship: Interpreting Christian Love*. Continuum, London, 2004. See also Donald Evans, *Spirituality and Human Nature*. State University of New York Press, Albany, N.Y., 1993, chapter II (on 'friendship-love').

5 The trials of a life

The second quotation at the head of the chapter is the last sentence of Anne Michaels' novel, *Fugitive Pieces*. Bloomsbury, London, 1996, p. 294. The quotation from Samuel Butler's satirical novel *Erewhon* (1872) is from chapter IV. John Keats rejected the use of the phrase 'vale of tears' with reference to our world, in favour of 'the vale of soul-making', in a letter reprinted in Grant F. Scott (ed.), *Selected Letters of John Keats*. Harvard University Press, Cambridge, Mass., 2002, pp. 290–2. John Hick's soul-making theodicy is briefly argued in his essay in Stephen T. Davis (ed.), *Encountering Evil: Live Options in Theodicy*. T. & T. Clark, Edinburgh,

1981 and Westminster John Knox Press, Louisville, Ky., 2001 (I quote from p. 50 of the earlier edition). For more detail, see *Evil and the God of Love*. Collins, London, 1968 (pp. 291 and 343 are quoted here). Anthony O'Hear's remarks are from *Experience, Explanation and Faith: An Introduction to the Philosophy of Religion*. Routledge & Kegan Paul, London, 1984, p. 211. Don Cupitt's radical response to the jibe that 'life is not fair' is from *Life, Life*. Polebridge Press, Santa Rosa, Calif., 2003, p. 58 (I later quote p. 137). Other quotations are from Keith Ward, *Divine Action*. London, Collins, 1990, p. 52; T. S. Eliot, 'Four Quartets: Little Gidding', IV, in his *Collected Poems 1909–1962*. Faber & Faber, London, and Harcourt Brace, Orlando, Florida, 1963, p. 221 (reproduced with permission); Holmes Rolston, *Science and Religion: A Critical Survey*. Random House, New York, 1987, p. 140; Daniel Migliore, *Faith Seeking Understanding: An Introduction to Christian Theology*. Eerdmans, Grand Rapids, Mich., 1991. pp. 116–17; and Karl Barth, *Church Dogmatics*, Vol. IV, Part 2. T. & T. Clark, Edinburgh, 1958, p. 469. 'Do not go gentle into that good night' is the title of Dylan Thomas' poem for his dying father (1951, published in Walford Davies (ed.), *Dylan Thomas: Selected Poems*. London, Dent, 1974, pp. 131–2). Harry Williams writes of 'active acceptance' in *True Resurrection*. Mitchell Beazley, London, 1972, pp. 160–5. D. Z. Phillips' radical account of prayer is from *The Concept of Prayer* (Routledge & Kegan Paul, London, 1965), p. 120, and his critique of evil as an opportunity for character development from *The Problem of Evil and the Problem of God*. SCM, London, 2004, pp. 57–8. The Bob Dylan lyric is from 'Not Dark Yet', in the album *Time Out of Mind* (Sony, 1997); his point seems to be more pessimistic than mine. I quote again Søren Kierkegaard, *Training in Christianity*. Princeton, N.J., Princeton University Press, 1941, pp. 171–3, 181–2, 220, 251–2.

Other things to read

Peter Vardy's *The Puzzle of Evil*, HarperCollins, London, 1992 is a good introduction to the problem of evil; chapters 6 and 7 of my *God's World* (Darton, Longman & Todd, London, 2000) deal with these matters much more briefly. Other accessible works on this theme include John Cottingham, *On the Meaning of Life*. Routledge, London, 2003, chapter 2; John Cowburn, SJ, *Shadows and the Dark: The Problems of Suffering and Evil*. SCM, London, 1979; Austin Farrer, *Love Almighty and Ills Unlimited*. Collins, London, 1962; and Brian Horne, *Imagining Evil*. Darton, Longman & Todd, London, 1996. Jeff Astley, David Brown and Ann Loades (eds), *Evil: A Reader*. T. & T. Clark, London, 2003 is an anthology of material on the problem of evil, drawn mainly from Christianity but also from some Jewish and Buddhist sources. More experiential and spiritual responses to suffering and bereavement include C. S. Lewis, *A Grief Observed*. Faber & Faber, London, 1961 and HarperSanFrancisco, San Francisco, 2001; David A. Pailin, *A Gentle Touch: From a Theology of Handicap to a Theology of Human Being*. SPCK, London, 1992; Margaret Spufford, *Celebration*. Mowbray, London, 1989; and Nicholas Wolterstorff, *Lament for a Son*. Eerdmans: Grand Rapids, Mich., 1987. See also Kenneth Leech, *We Preach Christ Crucified*. Darton, Longman & Todd, London, 2006.

6 Bearing all for joy

The first passage cited is from Austin Farrer, *The Brink of Mystery*. SPCK, London, 1976, pp. 67–8; the second is a verse from *The Nativity of Christ* by Robert Southwell. The quotation from the fifteenth-century German ascetical writer Thomas à Kempis is from his *Imitation of Christ*, book 2, chapter 12: 'Of the King's Highway of the Cross'. Apollinaire Guillaume's poem is 'Le Pont Mirabeau' (1912). I quote Robert C. Solomon, *The Passions: The Myth and Nature of Human Emotion*. University of Notre Dame Press, Notre Dame, Ind., 1976, pp. 133, 366–7. The quotation from John Barton is in *Living Belief: Being Christian and Being Human*. Continuum, London, 2005, p. 93. Some of my reflections on Cupitt are drawn from my article, 'Faith on the Level', *The Modern Churchman*. XXXII, 4, 1991, pp. 58–70. Quotations from Don Cupitt are from *The Time Being*. SCM, London, 1992, pp. 13, 61; *Solar Ethics*. SCM, London, 1995, pp. 19, 35; *After All: Religion Without Alienation*. SCM, London, 1994, pp. 81, 92, 94; *The New Christian Ethics*. SCM, London, 1988, pp. 98, 130, 167; *Philosophy's Own Religion*. SCM, London, 2000, p. 88; and *Emptiness and Brightness*. Polebridge Press, Santa Rosa, Calif., 2001, p. 51. 'Change and decay' is from Henry Francis Lyte's hymn, 'Abide with me' (1847). Iris Murdoch's account of the 'unselfing' power of Nature is from *The Sovereignty of Good*. Routledge & Kegan Paul, London, 1970, pp. 84–5; I also cite p. 52. I quote next from Craig Dykstra's, *Growing in the Life of Faith*. Geneva Press, Louisville, Ky., 1999, p. 90. *Surprised by Joy: The Shape of My Early Life* is C. S. Lewis' spiritual autobiography (published by Collins, London, 1959); William Wordsworth's poem, 'Surprised by joy – impatient as the wind' was written in 1815. I quote twice from Blake, from 'Eternity' and 'Auguries of innocence' (*Poems and Prophecies by William Blake*. Dent, London, 1927, pp. 383, 333). The quotation from Harry Williams is from *The Joy of God*. Mitchell Beazley, London, 1979, p. 50. Thomas Traherne's 'First century', written around 1672, is in his *Centuries of Meditations*; I quote from §25 and §28. Whitman's poem 'Miracles' is reprinted in *Walt Whitman: The Complete Poems*. Penguin, London, 1996, pp. 409–10. I quote Joachim Jeremias, 'The Lord's Prayer in Modern Research', in Richard Batey (ed.), *New Testament Issues*. SCM, London, 1970, pp. 98–9; George Eliot, *Middlemarch*. Penguin, London, 1994, p. 838; and J. D. Salinger, *Franny and Zooey*. Penguin, London, 1964, pp. 155–6.

Other things to read

Plato's account of appearance and reality is to be found in his *Republic*; see particularly the first part of book VII (chapter XXV in the Clarendon Press translation by F. M. Cornford, 1941). For more theological reflections on joy, see John Barton, *Living Belief*. London, Continuum, 2005, chapters 6–8, and Harry Williams, *The Joy of God*. Mitchell Beazley, London, 1979. For Harry Williams on the cross, see *God's Wisdom in Christ's Cross*. Mowbray, London, 1960. The ideas of 'biophilia', 'reconnecting with Nature' and 'ecopsychology' are often ridiculed, but they share a kinship with a creation-spirituality that also finds emotional healing in the contemplation of the natural world. See Edward O. Wilson, *The Diversity of Life*. Harvard University Press, Cambridge, Mass., 1992, pp. 349–51; Theodore Roszak, *The Voice of the Earth: An Exploration of Ecopsychology*. Simon & Schuster, New York, 1992; and Matthew Fox, *Creation Spirituality: Liberating Gifts for the Peoples of the Earth*. HarperCollins, New York, 1991. More mainstream theological reflections include Pierre Teilhard de Chardin, *Hymn of the*

Universe. Collins, London, 1965, and Celia Deane-Drummond, *Wonder and Wisdom: Conversations in Science, Spirituality and Theology*. Darton, Longman & Todd, London, 2006.

7 Beginning at the end

The verses at the head of the chapter form the last of Gordon Jackson's *Fifteen Lenten Sonnets: For Raphael Loewe*. Asgill Press, Lincoln, 2001, p. 19; reproduced with the author's kind permission. John Knox's book is *The Humanity and Divinity of Christ: A Study of Pattern in Christology*. Cambridge University Press, Cambridge, 1967. 'The carol' is by Christina Rossetti (1830–94). The survey is from Clive D. Field, '"It's all Chicks and Going Out": The Observance of Easter in Postwar Britain', *Theology*. CI, 800, 1998, pp. 82–90, and I quote T. S. Eliot, 'Little Gidding', section V from *Collected Poems 1909–1962*. Faber & Faber, London, 1963, p. 221 (reproduced with permission). Xenophanes and Timor of Phleios ('another critic') are quoted in Paul Feyerabend, 'Realism and the Historicity of Knowledge', *Journal of Philosophy*. LXXXVI, 8, 1989, p. 396. Rupert Brooke's poem was first published in 1915; A. D. Hope's 'The House of God' is reproduced by arrangement with the Licensor, the estate of A. D. Hope, c/o Curtis Brown (Aust.) Pty Ltd, from *Collected Poems 1930–1970*. Angus and Robertson, Sydney, 1972 (reprinted in D. J. Enright (ed.), *The Oxford Book of Contemporary Verse 1945–1980*. Oxford University Press, Oxford, 1980, pp. 18–19). The translation from Gustave Flaubert's *Madame Bovary* (1857, part 1, chapter 12) is by F. Steegmuller. Harry Williams' iconoclastic comment comes from *Some Day I'll Find You*. Collins, London, 1984, p. 127. I quote Kant's *Groundwork of the Metaphysic of Morals*, from H. J. Paton, *The Moral Law*. Hutchinson, London, 1948, p. 73; Basil Mitchell, *Morality: Religious and Secular – The Dilemma of Traditional Conscience*. Clarendon, Oxford, 1980, pp. 152–3; J. L. Houlden, *Jesus, A Question of Identity*. Continuum, London, 2006, p. 124; John Cottingham, *The Spiritual Dimension: Religion, Philosophy and Human Value*. Cambridge University Press, Cambridge, 2005, pp. 15–16; and Terrence W. Tilley, *Inventing Catholic Tradition*. Orbis, Maryknoll, N.Y., 2000, p. 112. 'Jesus foretold the kingdom . . .' is by Alfred Loisy (1857–1940). The gospel as 'the saltness of the salt' is a phrase from C. E. B. Cranfield, *The Gospel According to Saint Mark*. Cambridge University Press, Cambridge, 1977, p. 316. I quote Friedrich Nietzsche, *Thus Spake Zarathustra* (1883). Penguin, Harmondsworth, 1969, p. 213, and James M. Day, 'The Primacy of Relationship' in James C. Conroy (ed.), *Catholic Education: Inside-Out/Outside-In*. Veritas, Dublin, 1999, p. 280.

Other things to read

The spirituality and theology of resurrection are tackled in greater depth by Harry Williams, *True Resurrection*. Mitchell Beazley, London, 1972, and Rowan Williams, *Resurrection: Interpreting the Easter Gospel*. Darton, Longman & Todd, London, 2002. I have written on religious language in *Exploring God-Talk: Using Language in Religion*. Darton, Longman & Todd, London, 2004; and on the tension between religious tradition and contemporary experience in Jeff Astley and David Day (eds), *The Contours of Christian Education*. McCrimmons, Great Wakering, Essex, 1992, chapter 3. For reflections on the present state of the Church and its possible futures, see Steven Croft, *Transforming Communities: Re-Imagining the Church for the 21st Century*. Darton, Longman & Todd, London, 2002; John Drane, *The McDonaldization of the Church: Spirituality, Creativity, and the Future of the Church*. Darton, Longman & Todd, London, 2000; David Lyon, *Jesus in Disneyland: Religion in Postmodern Times*. Polity, Cambridge, 2000; and Pete Ward, *Liquid Church*. Paternoster, Carlisle, 2002. On welcoming a variety of views in religion, see Richard Holloway, *Doubts and Loves: What is Left of Christianity*. Canongate, Edinburgh, 2001. For more general works on the cultural and intellectual character of the age, see David Lyon, *Postmodernity*. Open University Press, Buckingham, 1994; Patricia Ward (ed.), *Postmodernism: A Reader*. Edward Arnold, London, 1992; or (if you like 'illustrated philosophy') Richard Appignanesi and Chris Garratt, *Postmodernism for Beginners*. Icon Books, Cambridge, 1995.

8 The multifaceted Jesus

The quotation from Hans Küng is from *On Being a Christian*. SCM, London, 1977, p. 125. I quote the 'one Jesus, many Christs' claim from

Don Cupitt's essay in S. W. Sykes and J. P. Clayton (eds), *Christ, Faith and History: Cambridge Studies in Christology*. Cambridge University Press, Cambridge, 1972, p. 143. The research on personality in Christology is reported in Leslie J. Francis and Jeff Astley, 'The Quest for the Psychological Jesus: Influences of Personality on Images of Jesus', *Journal of Psychology and Christianity*. 16, 3, 1997, pp. 247–59. I quote George Tyrrell, *Christianity at the Cross-Roads*. George Allen & Unwin, London, 1963 (originally published 1909), pp. 22 and 49; J. L. Houlden, *Jesus, A Question of Identity*. Continuum, London, 2006, p. 124; Albert Schweitzer, *The Quest of the Historical Jesus*. London, A. & C. Black, 1911, p. 4; Alain de Botton, *Status Anxiety*. Hamish Hamilton, London, 2004, p. 79; Joel B. Green in Markus Bockmuehl (ed.), *The Cambridge Companion to Jesus*. Cambridge University Press, Cambridge, 2001, pp. 93, 97; and Austin Farrer, *The Brink of Mystery*. SPCK, London, 1976, pp. 45–7.

Other things to read

Relatively readable general works on Christology include John Bowden, *Jesus: The Unanswered Questions*. SCM, London, 1988; Don Cupitt, *The Debate about Christ*. SCM, London, 1979; Jaroslav Pelikan, *Jesus through the Centuries: His Place in the History of Culture*. Harper & Row, New York, 1987; Geza Vermes, *The Changing Face of Jesus*. Penguin, London, 2001; N. T. Wright and Marcus Borg, *The Meaning of Jesus: Two Visions*. SPCK, London, 1999. See also John Dominic Crossan, *The Historical Jesus: The Life of a Mediterranean Jewish Peasant*. HarperSanFrancisco, New York, N.Y., 1992; J. L. Houlden, *Jesus, A Question of Identity* (details above); John Macquarrie, *Jesus Christ in Modern Thought*. SCM, London, 1990; and C. F. D. Moule, *The Origin of Christology*. Cambridge University Press, Cambridge, 1977. A classic – and still readable – account of the significance of parents in their children's Christian learning is Horace Bushnell, *Christian Nurture*. Baker Book House, Grand Rapids, Mich., 1979 (originally published 1861). For a similar viewpoint, see John H. Westerhoff, *Bringing Up Children in the Christian Faith*. Winston Press, Minneapolis, Minn., 2000.

Index of names

Abraham 43, 83
Adam 62–4, 78
Aelred, Abbot of Rievaulx 51–2, 133
Ammonas 35, 131
Andrew ix
Anglican 24, 38
Antony, St 28, 35
Appignanesi, Richard 139
Aquinas, Thomas 51, 133
Aristotle 42, 47, 134
Arnold, Matthew 34, 131
Aslan 32
Astley, Jeff 128, 129, 134, 136, 139, 140
Authorized Version 27, 98

Balfour, A. S. 56
Barth, Karl 7, 68, 129, 135
Barton, John 79, 136, 137
Batey, Richard 137
Blake, William 6, 84, 85, 129, 137
Bockmuehl, Markus 140
Book of Common Prayer (1662) 54
Borg, Marcus 140
Bowden, John 140
Brooke, Rupert 99, 138
Brown, Dan 20
Brown, David 136
Brownies 24
Buber, Martin 21, 130
Buddhism 83
Bushnell, Horace 140
Butler, Joseph 54, 133
Butler, Samuel 61, 134
Byatt, A. S. 130

Caesar 15
Caesarea Philippi 112
Carmichael, E. D. H. (Liz) 134
Carretto, Carlo 39, 132
Chapman, Graham 129
Chronicles, Second Book of 43
Clayton, J. P. 140
Cleese, John 11
Cohen, J. M. 133
Colossians, Letter to 103
Community of the Resurrection 28
Conroy, James C. 139
Corinthians, Letters to 17, 62, 70, 74, 94, 98, 103, 117–18
Cottingham, John 102, 135, 138
Cowburn, John 135–6
Craddock, Fred 128
Cranfield, C. E. B. 139
Croft, Steven 139
Crossan, John Dominic 140
Cupitt, Don 1, 65, 68, 79–83, 87–9, 113, 128, 129, 132, 135, 136, 140

David 44
Davies, Walford 135
Davis, Stephen T. 134–5
Day, David 128, 129, 134, 139
Day, James M. 110, 139
de Botton, Alain 19, 120, 130, 134, 140

de Caussade, Jean-Pierre 132
de Ganys, Bors 56
De Montaigne, Michel 49, 54, 133, 134
Deane-Drummond, Celia 138
Defoe, Daniel 62
Desert Fathers 28, 131, 132
Devil 12, 28, 62–3
Dickens, Charles 84
Dictionary of Christian Spirituality 43
Donne, John 41, 132
Drane, John 139
Drury, John 129
Dryden, John 42, 133
Dykstra, Craig 10, 81, 129, 137
Dylan, Bob 71, 130, 135

Ecclesiasticus 49
Ecclestone, Alan 132
Egypt 40
Eliot, George 87, 137
Eliot, T. S. 67, 96, 130, 135, 138
Emerson, Ralph Waldo 42, 47–8, 54, 56, 57, 132–3
Emmaus 94
Enright, D. J. 132, 138
Ephesians, Letter to 9, 103
Epicurus 134
Evans, Donald 48–51, 133, 134
Eve 64

141

Index of names

Naomi 44
Nietzsche, Friedrich 109, 139
Nouwen, Henri J. M. 35, 131–2

Oates, Mightily 21
O'Hear, Anthony 65, 135
Oxford Dictionary of the Christian Church, The 43

Pailin, David A. 136
Palmer, Parker J. 28, 131
Panichas, George A. 133
Paton, H. J. 138
Paul, St 13, 70, 75, 94, 117–18
Pelikan, Jaroslav 140
Peter, St 102, 117; Simon [Peter] ix
Philippians, Letter to 13, 121
Phillips, Dewi Z. 68–9, 135
Plato 82, 137
Pratchett, Terry 21, 130
Price, H. H. 50, 133
Prince of Wales 28
Procrustes/Procrustean 33–4
Proverbs, Book of 43–4
Psalms, Book of 26, 43, 59–60, 63, 79, 123

Rankin, W. M. 133
Rengstorf, K. H. 129
Revised Standard Version (Bible) 16
Rice, Tim 46, 133
Richter, Philip 24, 130
Rolston, Holmes 67, 135
Romans, Letter to 75
Rome/Romans 12, 124
Rossetti, Christina 138

Roszak, Theodore 137
Russell, Willy 36
Ruth 44

Sahara 39
Salinger, J. D. 137
Samuel, Books of 17, 44
Satan 27, 29, 62–3
Saul, King 44
Schweitzer, Albert 115, 140
Scott, Grant F. 134
Scrooge, Ebenezer 84
Sirach 49
Society of Friends (the Quakers) 43
Sodom 83
Solomon, Robert C. 77–8, 136
Sounes, Howard 130
Southwell, Robert 52, 74, 133, 136
Spencer, Diana 28
Spohn, William C. 25, 130
Spufford, Margaret 136
Stählin, Gustav 43–4, 133
Steegmuller, F. 138
Stevens, George 94
Sykes, S. W. 140
Synoptic Gospels 45

Teilhard de Chardin, Pierre 137–8
Teletubbies 18
Teresa of Avila, St 55, 133
Thomas, Dylan 135
Thomas, Kunjana 132
Thomas, R. S. 38, 132
Tiberius Caesar Augustus 15
Tilley, Terrence W. 106, 138
Timor of Phleios 138
Traherne, Thomas 85–6, 137

Tyrrell, George 114–15, 140

Valentine, Shirley 36
Vardy, Peter 134, 135
Vermes, Geza 140

Wakefield, Gordon S. 131
Ward, Benedicta 132
Ward, Keith 66, 135
Ward, Patricia 139
Ward, Pete 139
Warhol, Andy 18
Weatherwax, Granny 21
Weil, Simone 57, 133
Wesley, John 31, 131
Westerhoff, John H. 140
Whitehead, Alfred North 32, 131
Whitman, Walt 55, 85, 133, 137
Williams, Harry 28–30, 36, 40, 68, 76, 85, 101, 131, 132, 135, 137, 138, 139
Williams, Mark F. 133
Williams, Rowan 28, 131, 132, 139
Wilson, A. N. 27, 131
Wilson, Edward O. 82, 137
Wittgenstein, Ludwig 4, 129
Wolterstorff, Nicholas 136
Wordsworth, William 30, 84, 131, 137
Wright, N. T. 140

Xenophanes of Colophon 97–9, 138

Zacchaeus 20, 118–19
Zarathustra/Zoroastrian 109
Zohar, Danah 130

143

Index of themes

——◆◆——

Index of themes

Index of themes

relativism 49, 53, 97–102, 112–19; *see also* personal
religious experience 5–6, 36–7, 80–1, 82; *see also* vision, spiritual
respect 12, 19, 21–2, 50, 51, 55, 62, 113
resurrection 76, 92–111, 120–1
revelation 1, 4, 37, 40, 53, 80, 100, 110
rich 21
road x, ix, 2, 9–14, 48, 58, 94–5, 109, 111, 116–17, 127; *see also* following; journey; way

sacrament 4, 86
saints/sainthood 22–3, 25, 35, 46
salt 107–8
salvific 109, 116, 118–19, 125
Satan 27–30, 62–3
scandal of Jesus 20
second coming 111
seeing *see* vision, spiritual
self-interest 49–51, 55–6; *see also* unselfing
self-righteousness 65
silence 28, 35–9, 89, 122; hearing the 37–8
sin/sinner 4, 12–13, 20–3, 25, 27, 33, 44, 46, 59, 62, 77–8, 104, 118–19, 127
society 31–2

solitude *see* alone
soul-making 63–5, 69–70
Spirit/Holy Spirit 27, 30, 51, 103
spiritual change *see* spirituality; change
spiritual growth *see* learning Christ; soul-making
spirituality 4–7, 67–73, 80–90; *see also* ordinary spirituality/theology; vision, spiritual; and *passim*
status 12–13, 18–19, 24, 87–90, 120–7; status anxiety 19, 130
success 6, 15, 19, 34, 59, 71, 77, 122–3
suffering 25–6, 58–73; acceptance of and resistance to 67–72; gratuity of 64–5; meaning of 70–3; mystery of 64–5; and spirituality 67–73
superficiality xi, 7, 19–26, 82, 92, 95–6, 104; *see also* depth; point, seeing
surfaces *see* superficiality

tax collectors 12–13, 20, 118
theology 98: anecdotal xiii; ordinary *see* ordinary spirituality/ theology

thinking *see* reason
transient/transitory 79–80, 83–5
trial 58–73; definition of 58–9
truth xii, 4, 9, 14, 22, 26, 28, 37, 47–9, 72, 97, 101–2, 109–10, 119

uniformity 34; *see also* individuality/ individuals
unselfing 81

value-raising/valuing xi–xiii, 2, 16–24, 49, 50, 53, 71, 83, 87–9, 97, 101–2, 113–27
values, learning 126
vision, spiritual xi, 4–7, 11–14, 16–18, 29, 69, 85, 92, 112–17, 120
vulnerability 10–11, 67, 124

way ix–xiv, 1–14, 58, 108–10, 117, 127; *see also* following; journey; road
well, metaphor of 114–16
widow's mite 4, 24, 70, 122
wilderness *see* desert
wisdom 17–18, 68–70, 127
work 2, 26, 29, 39, 111
worship 113, 116

yeast 107–8